REAL WEALTH AND ECONOMIC CLIMATE CHANGE

Copyright 2025 by Author
Bobby Dee Ticer

Table of Contents

Preface	3 5
1. Introduction	12
2. Rise of Civilization	22
3. Political Economic History of Europe	32
4. Democratic Republic of American	38
5. Bank America	44
6. Slavery Controversy and Civil War	52
7. Change and Adjustment Economics	62
8. Thrue Economics and Real Wealth	74
9. Natural Cycles or Industrial Causes to Climate Change	82
10. Investing for Climate Change	96
11. A Population Issue of Concern	100
My Health on Earth	

Disclaimer

This book is merely an attempt to contribute to the need of reversing dramatic effects of climate change. It is only in support instead of a challenge to any other attempt.

PREFACE

What is the economic value of the air we breathe?

Since it is free to breathe, it has no economic value other than negative ones to whomever there is cost to overcome such costly effects as predicted to occur of climate change. Such cost is either social cooperation or of individual competition depending on whether individuals or government pays for either recovery or prevention of damage. Prevention of climate change is more social in the sense of it requiring changeover from fossil to clean energy fuels. Whereas fossil fuels are competitively of free enterprise, social compromise is generally required for the promotion of clean energy, which has tremendous resistance to those in favor of the former. Even investors in fossil fuel stocks tend to oppose changeover to clean energy alternatives. However, government military to defend free enterprise from invasion by another nation is social as well with nearly total approval.

A means of overcoming resistance to fossil fuels could be promotion of how investment in clean energy solutions provide more opportunity for individuals to achieve more economic wealth, such as if only by means of stock purchase. With extreme damage of more hazardous conditions of climate change, higher insurance rates along with more rebuilding could result in more investment failure, whereas companies around the world in support of combating such hazards have been becoming more successful of late as a more successful means of future investment.

There are many books published about economic climate change. The intent of this one is neither to challenge nor compete against any of them. It is merely an attempt to be another contributor in the sense of helping promote truth of what can be done to prevent the hazardous conditions of climate change. Argument against social aspects of society is that being in government control by means of vote by the general public might not be intelligent enough to decide the best way forward, even though the opposite policy of dictatorship has often led to such undesirable outcomes as citizens becoming slaves to dictatorship. Truth can be a contributor to success, and education by either self-experience or academic research is a practical means of attaining it.

Knowledge is a key factor of issue. Examples are of sports. The more ways you know how to execute ways to win generally results in more success. However, it can also be subjective in the sense that what works for one person or team might not work as well for another.

Even though the historical development of civilization and its economics is more subjective, learning from experience and schooling has resulted in more prosperous ways of overcoming changes in more prosperous ways. The intent of this book is to display them in hope voters can be more inclined to know truthfulness of their votes along with how they can contribute to a healthier environment. However, it is just a single effort of partial contribution in view of much more needed success. There are such other contributors as Exxon Mobile that seems to be making substantial progress. This author has no affiliation whatsoever with it or any other contributor. He just recognizes it as a particular pathway of investing by way of either the stock market or developmental participation. Owners of fossil fuel stocks could thus have a way to reinvest in clean energy initiatives as a practical means of avoiding bankrupt by being able to transfer over to cleaner energy production increasing more of its future value.

More knowledge of the historical development of civilization is mainly just indication of how we humans along with other animals have developed by means of both individual competition and social cooperation. Such development is similar to learning by means of trial and error, as learning from our mistakes to achieve such more favorable outcomes as preventing self-destruction of war. Climate change is merely another hurdle to overcome. It has been becoming more of a world threat requiring social cooperation of nations as well as their individual civilians. Those in favor of it promoting use of cleaner and freer energies could eventually become more prosperous.

1
INTRODUCTION

Proposed solutions of climate change are generally subjective inasmuch as what is right for me might not be right for you. One of us might benefit from digestion of an apple and the other from digestion of an orange. This author generally consumed an apple regularly in the morning. One morning he further consumed an orange after less than an hour after consuming an apple, became plugged up and had to get off the bus to throw up. Another person might be more adapted to the consumption of the orange than the apple at some particular time. A particular person noted he had been eating apples and oranges regularly without ill-related side effects. Similarly, saliva tends to thicken where pollen occurs only in the spring and early summer whereas such effects seem less attainable in places where pollen occurs throughout the year. More adaptation can occur with longer time to adjust.

Change itself is an issue of concern. It might take some amount of time for the body to adjust to the consumption of either an orange or apple. Adjustment to financial conditions is also of economic concern. Creating a highway nearby a store could result in customers shopping somewhere else. Sufficient notification of the change might on the average allow store owners time to adjust by means of relocation.

Success of government investment generally requires ample time for adjusting to the change occurring from it. There is need to overcome climate change. However, converting directly to clean energy fuel could result in poverty of fossil fuel producers and other disasters if done with not enough time for adjustment. However, no willingness to change can also result in more drastic poverty for resisting proposed efforts assuring a healthier climate in which to live.

General benefits have occurred of such government investment as highways, schools and railroads. Schools have educated citizens for them to have more ability for more creative production of preferred products. It could be why the United States of American had during a particular time excelled economically more than almost every other nation, but there remain such economic issues of concern as inflation occurring from too much government investment.

What causes inflation?

It is generally explained according to supply and demand. More demand of less supply generally results in higher priced products whereas more supply on the open market having less demand generally results in lower prices, or even bankruptcy due to higher cost of production. For government investment to be successful, it needs to result in more products of more demand usually durable an ample time for feasible adjustment. It is also noted that people having more money to spend can also result in inflation. Government increasing money supply instead of taxation to invest in such policies as social security is subject to inflation if there is not enough increase in desirable products to purchase. There is nonetheless the possibility of increasing wealth by means of investment. Its result just needs to be of proper method for it to become successful in an ample amount of time. However, it can also be argued that it could also be needed to counter a negative effect occurring of natural change

Climate change is a critical issue of concern. The occurrence of global warming, as claimed according to authorities of advanced studies, could be extremely destructive to Earth's environment. There is negative change needing positive change instead in order for either maintaining a better economy or even creating more prosperity. However, there is also plenty of resistance to such change by the present establishment having less control of its production capability. If the production of fuel for automobiles becomes that of wind and solar energy, then producers of carbon fuels could become bankrupt.

Positive change is best done in correct manner for it to be more easily successful in due time with more general support. In general, too much change per time results in negative consequences even though positive results occur after much longer time periods.

Social capitalism might seem to be a contradiction in the sense capitalism generally connotes free choice for individual innovation to achieve economic success whereas social capitalism is according to majority rule in relation to majority vote by eligible citizens. However, there are many aspects of economics whereby social agreement is complementary to individual determination of it that promotes freedom in the form of more economic opportunity.

There is social tax for construction of roads and highways that provide more efficient transportation of goods and services. Even if they promote prosperity for both the rich and poor by allowing more transport of goods and services, larger corporations could have an advantage being that it is cheaper on the average for them to transport goods in larger bulk whereby fewer owners capitalize on their products. Smaller local companies have thus had less advantage of adjusting to government creation of highways and roads.

As for an example, there were gasoline wars in the 1950s. Although the price of gasoline was lowered to nineteen cents a gallon, it allowed larger national oil companies to sell at a lower price to eliminate competition of smaller local ones. Larger ones were somewhat able to raise prices after the elimination of its smaller competitors. In another sense, it has taken time for economic adjustment to occur among the more general society that has relatively become more dependent on larger companies fewer in number.

Results of adjustment further relate to acceptance. Success of larger companies is inclined to be more acceptable in the sense they provide more desirable products at less cost, but they could be less desirable by having an advantage over smaller competitors if too much unemployment occurs.

Construction of roads has been an overall benefit for the transport of more wealth even though it did provide an advantage to more wealthy producers of it. It is just a matter of how competitors are more able to adjust to change. Although more wealthy competitors might have an advantage in applying innovative ways for even more success, they could still be challenged by challengers creating more desirable products.

Another social means of success is freer education for those of us able to take advantage of it. Knowing the natural laws of physics, for instance, can benefit billiard players. Those of them with a better game plan and ability to apply what they know usually win more often. For example, knowing that stroking a pool stick straight at the cue ball's center is a necessary means of having a more accurate stroke, but knowing what results by not hitting the cue ball at its center provides more strategic ways for a successful game plan.

Controversy applies to the use of such terms as liberalism and conservatism. To the extreme right, conservatives do not want to allow change to occur. The wealthy thus tend to maintain in control by both political and economic persuasion. To the extreme left, liberals want social changes to occur in a way that they tend to result in a recession of the economy. In between extreme conservatism and liberalism can be compromised whereby debate can result in more understanding of how compromise can benefit the poor without resulting in lower wealth of the overall economy.

An essential example of opposition to change relates to deniers of climate change. Even though it has been predicted by climatologists that the excessive use of fossil fuel raises climate temperature and causes worldwide destruction, political deniers have been successful in denying a conversion to cleaner energy. Solutions are subjective in the sense it is natural for deniers of them insisting to maintain their right to compete according to established law. However, it is also natural for those more harshly affected by climate change to advocate more social change to combat it. Right or wrong, it is the intent of this book only to consider more ways for how reversing climate change can succeed in a more positive manner. It is mainly an historical review of how civilization has developed by means of both individual competition and social cooperation.

What is the economic value of the air we breathe?

With it being plentiful and immediately available, there is no positive economic value even though we are unable to live without it. The non-positive value is because of it being free to breathe. Similarly, blackberries in the Willamette Valley of Oregon seemingly have no economic value since they grow independently in abundance and tend to takeover. Even though they have nutritional benefits, they are merely considered to be weeds instead with a negative value for the difficulty of removing their thorny vines.

There is negative economic value to consider regarding cost of removing blackberries and overcoming massive damage due to climate change. As with the blackberries, victims of it are responsible for its presence. As with climate change, victims of it are a lot less responsible for its occurrence, as being individually able to partially prevent it if at all. However, there could be ways investment in clean energy could be more profitable to the overall economy.

Construction of highways has allowed for the transport of more wealth even though it has also allowed more successful enterprise to be more in control of it, and it also has social advantage inasmuch as it allows such prevention of destruction from forest fires and so forth. Similarly, taxation for military and police is acceptable for law and order and protection against invasion by another nation. However, the threat of climate change has been less acceptable. The reason for this lesser acceptability is subjectively more complex, but the overwhelming evidence of vast destruction caused by more heat in the atmosphere has been providing more incentive for combating the threats of climate change.

Freedom for obtaining the American Dream is also an issue of concern, but using it to combat the truth of climate change can result in less wealth of the general economy. The acceptance of truth is necessary to determine how such threats can be overcome. Because the general population has a say in the debate, they can help determine the result. However, the success of the debate depends on knowledge being truthful information of its participants. It also depends on positive outcomes, as in ways that benefit the general wealth of the public.

The main objective of this book is for understanding how overcoming climate change can be prosperous according to individual opportunity for investment. Understanding includes a historical background of civilization itself developed as economically more prosperous. Such accepted policies as the gold standard establishment in the past and as to why it no longer exists is to be understood within this context.

Chapter 2, titled Rise of Civilization, is a review of the historical beginning of civilization. It has significance in the sense of its having had innovative ways of creating more wealth in a social manner according to the needs of a growing population with better interaction among itself along with the development of agriculture along with law-and-order. More cooperative change occurred with agricultural development in contrast to more competitiveness of merely surviving by means of hunting and killing animals for food. The latter even provided more incentive to kill other humans to satisfy those more in need.

Chapter 3, titled Political Economic History of Europe, includes how the gold standard developed along with slavery and war. There were debates about laissez faire economic wealth opposing government interference in the open market. Further concerns were about mercantilism to maximize exports and minimize imports, and physiocracy believing government policy should not interfere with the nature of agriculture and its economics as natural laws. Along with trade, slavery became a particular way of obtaining an advantage over other nations even though competitive freedom became theorized as well. Social cooperation among nations as well as among people seems to have been in more need.

Chapter 4, titled Democratic Republic of America, is about why and how the USA became independent from the control of England. England was in control of trade policy according to ownership and payment by its own gold standard rules, but its colonies were in need of adjusting to their own particular circumstances.

Chapter 5, titled Bank America, is about how the banking system developed in the USA after it gained independence from England. There was debate concerning whether it should be either independent or of government control. Circumstances for survival and development were somewhat variable and complex.

Chapter 6, titled Slavery Controversy and Civil War, is also about economic circumstances. They were of critical outcome. Northerners opposed slavery because of it having advantage of trade imbalance regarding shipping of products to and from Europe, but they also had an advantage of being in control of shipping trade with other nations.

Chapter 7, titled Change and Adjustment Economics, is more about how the national banking system developed according to particular circumstances. The gold standard had developed along with the USA as one of its members, but trade along with other circumstance resulted in the Great Depression and World War II. Nations not abiding by the gold standard suffered less economic depression. Nations temporally departing from the gold standard generally recovered sooner. Eventually the USA permanently departed altogether from the Gold Standard.

Chapter 8, titled True Economics and Real Wealth, explains different ways of how monetary supply effects social needs and free enterprise. Devastations of climate change are prime examples.

Chapter 9, titled Natural Cycles or Industrial Causes of Climate Change, explains more in depth causes of climate change effects. Natural cycles occur of weather patterns along with the use of fossil fuels.

Chapter 10, titled Investing for Climate Change Solutions, proposes possible solutions to climate change in way of increasing prosperity of the overall economy. However, it in itself is not a total solution. Many other solutions are still needed, and this one only contributes.

2
RISE OF CIVILIZATION

Early rise of civilization is relevant insofar as it involves unity and conflict of people adapting to new forces of nature. It was influenced by a declining ice age from which sea levels about eleven thousand years ago were about three hundred feet lower than today's present levels. Floods followed along with the development of agriculture and larger communities of people.

As other animals compete to survive hazardous threats of life from either other animals or environmental conditions, we humans also have a tendency to deceive, steal and kill for enhancing our lives, but as some other animals also do, we unite together in order to survive more overbearing hazards confronting us. For instance, the flooding of plains became another challenge to survive. They influenced people to join together in order to overcome hazardous elements of nature in allowing us more freedom to develop individual efforts to gain in economic prosperity. Farming thus became a prosperous way of life. However, we humans are also inclined to become ruthless warriors in order to compete against ourselves to survive and prosper even more. Hunting behavior of cavemen thus remained part of our cultural behavior and traditional tendency.

It is evident we have evolved from being prehuman, which is prehistory in the sense established history is documented by writing preserved on stone tablets. Nonetheless, there is still a log of archaeological knowledge uncovered of our prehistory indicating how our civilization has evolved by innovative ways to overcome diversity.

Such cultural aspects of individualism likely dominated in slavery and war in both prehistory and early history. There has been a gradual change with population growth of farming communities and political economics. In the United States of America, for instance, women and negroes have eventually acquired equal and full citizenship.

At the peak of the last ice age occurring around 18,000 BC the climate was generally cooler in the northern hemisphere. The warming that followed was gradual, but it brought about more rainfall along with melting of glaciers. Some valleys were either permanently flooded or frequently flooded. The Mesopotamian Valley north of the Persian Gulf, for instance, was not inhabitable on a permanent basis until about 5000 BC even though agricultural settlements were established in the southern part of Asia before 8000 BC.

There was extensive development here and there. The oldest known grave site dates back to about 7000 BC at a location that is now Latvia bordering the Baltic Sea along with Sweden. Settlements also occurred during that century in the Zagros Mountains where what is now southwestern Iran. Another ancient settlement about that time was Jericho located north of the Dead Sea (Sea of Salt) that borders between eastern Jordan and western Israel, and it is now about eight hundred feet below sea level.

Although no grave site has been found as evidence of a first permanent settlement at Jerico, there was a massive wall twelve feet high surrounding it, most likely for protection against flooding and/or an invasion from other people. The initial settlement lasted a few centuries before being invaded by people who ruled over the people of the initial settlement. More ruling settlements followed.

Settlements also occurred during that century in the Zagros mountains where what is now southwestern Iran. Various sites of farming communities date as far back as about 8000 BC. They were located in the foothills of northern Mesopotamia beside the Zagros mountains of Iran.

Archaeologists of India have claimed to have found evidence of an early civilization having existed in the Indus valley where it is now parts of northwestern India, Pakistan and Afghanistan. There is evidence of large-scale structures with the wood being carbon dated farther back than the seventh millennium BC. Archaeologists also claim it is evident a civilization once existed about 7500 BC along the Gulf of Cambay (now referred to as Gulf of Khambhat) that is an inlet of the Arabian Sea at the west coast of India.

The origin and destiny of these people are not established, but the civilization is believed to have been a victim of catastrophic flooding, and there is one theory proposing that some of the people survived as the origin of Sumerians in southern Mesopotamia.

The origin of the Sumerians is also not established. A likely possibility proposed by Ashok Malhotra and other historians is that they migrated from the Indus Valley. Evidence is claimed in that there appears to be similarities of skeletons of ancient tribes in the Indus valley whereby ancient people living farther southeast nearer to Australia and having a language similar to ancient Sumerian culture could have migrated to Samaria. Although the evidence for this theory is not conclusive, with the original language of these earlier people having been erased by centuries of dominant development of other languages, the Sumerian literature did contain remarks of catastrophic flooding along with knowledge of the seas, and the Indus Valley has still been prone to flooding in more than twelve percent of India.
It appears that in ancient times the melting of glaciers in the

Himalayas resulted in a greater amount of flooding. Satellite images support Vedic claims that a gigantic river once existed. Moreover, the largest civilization during its times is believed to have existed in the Indus Valley of India and Pakistan where it is possible a southern sea people survived an enormous flood to migrate along the coastline of the Arabian Sea into the Persian Gulf toward a drier land just west of the Mesopotamian valley.

From that drier land they eventually migrated to Sameria when it finally became inhabitable on a permanent basis about 6000 BC. They first spoke an agglutinate language containing one syllable words combining in ways that do not lose individual meaning. About 5500 BC they further developed writing and pioneered the growing of grains. About 4800 BC they developed canals for the irrigation of agriculture. More social cooperation thus emerged.

People making eloquent pottery lived in foothills east of the Tigris River and Sameria where what is now southwestern Iran. The area was inhabited as early as 7000 BC. Such city states as one called Susa had emerged about 4000 BC. According to their own language, people called themselves Hartmut, but much later, according to another language, they are identified as Elamites of Elam.

Elamites differed from the people of that other language who were a later combination of Sumerians of different peoples in the southern part of Iraq. They had combined by means of Akkadians from norther Mesopotamia invading the Sumerians in the south.

There is also a reference to a possible Susa being Shushan in the Hebrew bible. It is noted that a biblical Elam was the son of Shem and a grandson of Noah. However, ancient names were also meaningful titles in contrast to surnames of today, and their origins are confusingly complex. According to the Semitic language of Akkadians, for instance, Elam meant highland. Similarly, people living in the southern part of Mesopotamia that are historically known as Sumerians had also obtained their name from the Akkadians, but the name Akkad itself is not of Akkadian origin. The Sumerians were a mixture of Bolivians as previous occupants of the city of Ubaid, and the Akkadians of Semitic origin described themselves as having dark heads, whether that meant just brunettes or dark skin people.

The Akkadian language as a variant of the Semitic language does not prevail in the same context of more modern literature. Mesopotamia itself is a Greek word Greeks had used to refer to the valley between the Euphrates and Tigris fivers, and the name Greek derives from the Latin name Graecia by means of Romans naming of a tribe of Hellenic people living in Epirus. The Greeks referred to themselves as Hellenes. History in accordance with language is thus more complex. Nonetheless, Genesis 10:10 of the bible states Nimrod was king or lord of Adda, and hundreds of documents have been found in both Sumerian and Akkadian languages in support of its truth.

Farming communities began emerging about 6500 BC in the norther region of Mesopotamia as well as in its southern region. It is believed people residing in the north generally spoke a language of Semitic origin, possibly as part of the more general groups of such later people becoming known as Subarians, Amorites, Akkadians, Assyrians and Hittites.

It is also evident a culture of people called Badari settled along the eastern shore and southern part of the Nile River about 5000 BC to live on a diet of wheat, barley, lentils, tubers, fish and animals. Pits indicate the use of granaries. Smoking of fish is also indicated as a method of preservation.

Large pottery too fragile to transport further indicates permanent but smaller settlements. Their tools included scraper and axes. Domestication of animals included cattle, sheep, goats and dogs. The latter are now believed to have evolved from wolves in northeast China at least as far back as about 15,000 years ago. Because such wolf-like instincts were still among them as stalking of prey, they became herders of sheep that bundled for self-protection. Barking dogs also warned against the intrusions of enemies.

Badarian people were not isolated. They traded with surrounding people whereby elephant ivory most likely was acquired south of Badari. They also obtained copper from northern areas. However, peaceful trade is not indicative in all respects. Injuries of the people, evident from skeletons found at their grave sites, indicate competitive conditions of survival from either hazardous climate, confrontation among themselves, or confrontation with other people.

War might have originated as a means of survival. People settled in the fertile valleys relatively having more resources to such essential means of survival as food. They expanded their wealth by means of canals to extend the water supply to arid regions. However, with increase in population and more extreme drought, there became have and have-nots. If those having wealth did not protect it, they were subject to conquest by other people in need of it. Even if not in need, conquest of other people could have a competitive means of gaining control even if only for power of control.

With advance of civilization during the Bronze age, spoils of war became more enticing. If people did not share their wealth, revolution or just plain war itself could have been more inevitable as an alternative means of survival. Those who competed against harsher conditions in order to survive were likely inclined to survive a harsher nature, and leaders of the wealthy likely became ruthless to maintain their role of leadership to secure it against a coupe. People in fear of change and conquest are also more likely to support a stronger leader no matter how ruthless the leader might be.

Along with the development of nations, greater weaponry along with economic wealth and competition among leaders likely escalated for the dominance of power. However, friendly trade among nations escalated as well. Both trends are still evident in modern times.

An early Bronze age began developing in the middle east around 3300 BC, but tin from there contained arsenic. The alloying of tin with copper resulted in a toxic bronze. A non-toxic tin was thus needed for it to smelt with copper to produce a healthier bronze alloy. The non-toxic tin came later from European areas of Spain, England, France and Portugal about 2000 BC. Evidence from sunken ships found in the Mediterranean Sea indicates a trade route existed from those areas to Egypt and Mesopotamia.

The advanced civilizations of Mesopotamia and Egypt became central to trade. The name Egypt was also not original. It derives from a later time of Greek mythology whereby Aegyptus was the king of Aradia and Egypt. Ancient Egypt was previously known as the land of Kemet, meaning the land of dark soil. It might have received its new name because of a flooding of the river Nile over the land to fertilize it with a soil silt rich in nutrients.

Along with trade were developments of communication, government, writing and so forth. Earliest writing in Egypt was pictograph. Other writing developed independently here and there, as in China, Europe, Asia Minor, the Indus Valley, Crete and Mesopotamia. The Sumerians seem to have advanced it sooner prior to the Bronze Age. Their language was a cuneiform script. During the third millennium BC the pictographs at Sameria developed into a symbolic script that continually became refined of less symbols with more general abstract meanings. However, they did not develop an alphabet. The first known alphabet has been credited to the Phoenicians who became very prosperous during the Bronze age as a maritime civilization.

The Phoenicians from the city known to them as Sidon called themselves Sidonians. They might have originated the name Phoenician in honor of a king named Phoenix. Another possibility is that Sidonians were called by Greeks the Phoenicians because they sold a purple dye made from oyster shells. They are associated with Canaanite people that inhabited the area of Lebanon, Israel, Palestine, West Ordan and Southwest Syria. Canaan also had a Hurrian Semitic meaning similar to that of the Greek meaning of Phoenicia referring to people who produced and exported purple cloth that could have become the naming of a city selling it, and the Phoenician maritime empire of cities centered along the Mediterranean coast near Lebanon and Syria.
Phoenicians, no matter what was the origin of their name, thus became the primary instruments of trade and commerce in the middle east by means of the seas.

The advancement of civilization was classified in relation to the Bronze age by the historian Christian Jurgensen Thomsen that began in Egypt about 3150 BC with a north-south unification occurring about 3100 BC and the building of the Great Pyramid of Giza being completed about 2560 BC. A middle Bronze age is claimed to have occurred from about 2055 to 1650 BC followed by a late Bronze age in the sixteenth century BC that lasted on into the eleventh century BC.

The Bronze age extended into Europe from such development of civilization on such Mediterranean islands as Crete where the Bronze age began about 3000 BC. Stone tools have been found on Crete dating as far back as one-hundred and thirty thousand years. It could indicate the use of boats, but the sea levels were much lower that far back in the past. Modern human population only dates back to about ten-thousand BC. A Minoan civilization, named after a legendary ruler Minos of the city Knossos, flourished during the Bronze age from about 3500 BC to 1100 BC. An original script, linear A, was found on it that has not been deciphered because of there being no similarity of it to a Rosetta stone that was found containing both Egyptian and Greek script, but a later linear B script of a combination of Minoan and Greek language was found.

Although the island was ravaged by a volcano, earthquake and tsunamis, it flourished between 2700 BC and 1450 BC. Such extensive waterways as aqueducts were built along with three story buildings and palaces having running water to drink and clean with. Cisterns collected water from flat roofs. Water was even treated by flowing through a porous clay pipe. Cattle, sheep, goats and pigs were some of the domesticated animals raised. Diets included grapes, figs, olives, lettuce, celery, pears and fish.

The rise of civilization brought about both prosperity and conflict. As an analogical example, consider the nature of penguins on the continent of Antarctica. During freezing winter, they are socially cooperative in bundling together. Because penguins near center become too warm, they go outside to cool off while the rest of them close inward for having more warmth, thus creating a natural cycle for preservation. During springtime, males and females are cooperative in taking turns protecting eggs while the other goes to the ocean for food. However, some penguins cheat on their mates in causing confrontations. When eggs hatch into young penguins, they are cared for by their parents, but when the young ones finally begin to explore on their own, they are harassed by older penguins protecting their territories to sometimes even kill intruders.

We are also animals. We group together for protection and build walls among ourselves. We devise rules of conduct in order to live in harmony. However, we also compete for survival. Leadership occurs whether it is for control by means of war or for peaceful tranquility and prosperity.

For the sake of economic wealth and its security, imperialism became a common objective. A Babylonian empire was an early leader of this quest. Babylon was a city of the Akkadian empire established about 2300 BC. In 1792 BC, Hammurabi became the ruler. He established a law code mostly in context of an eye for an eye. For instance, if a son was killed, the father was given permission to kill a son of the killer. If a physician failed to save the life of a slave of a freeman, the physician was required to replace the slave with another slave.

The Babylonian empire entailed the conquest of the southern part of Mesopotamia before conquering all of it. It continued with the conquest of the Elamites, Gutians, Kassites, Semitic states (Syria) and Asia Minor (Turkey). After Hammurabi died in 1750 BC, the empire crumbled due to internal conflict for power and control.

The demise of the Babylonian empire is typified by the last king of Ur, Ibbi-Sin, who succeeded his father Shu-sin about 1964 BC. Shu-sin had about a hundred-and-seventy-mile-long wall constructed between the Tigris and Euphrates rivers. It was supposed to keep out the Assyrians who were experiencing a long drought. The wall was not a successful preventative. Ur was overpowered. Arid land is still a problem in relation to drought and not enough food to feed its population, and more remedies besides a wall are needed to solve problems of people attempting to migrate from grave conditions. Instead of building walls for distribution of wealth being controlled by a nation of more favorable wealth, a better option could be a world organization to combat drought and climate change in a way there is feasible distribution of wealth for all of us to succeed and contribute to economic prosperity, peace and world order.

The Persian empire ruled by Cyrus the Great dominated about 550 BC. It originated in the northern part of Iran and extended to its southern part into Anatolia (Turkey), Egypt, northern India and central Asia. It weakened with its attempt to conquer what is now Greece, which later became dominate under the rule of Alexander the Great.

Later empires were the Roman, Napoleonic and British. A later failure was the attempt of Adolf Hitler. Subsequent possible dominance has been thwarted by a nuclear threat of the capability of destroying the other as well civilization in general.

Customs have been a means of preferred behavior. Some of them have originated before the beginning of civilization. They have resulted in both economic innovation and wars for the control of wealth. Archaeologists also claim it is evident a civilization of people once existed about 7500 BC along the Gulf of Cambay that is an inlet of the Arabian Sea at the west coast of India. A laissez-faire wealth of France was based on agriculture. The mercantile wealth of England was based on gold and the manufacturing of wealth. In the United States, there was sort of a north and south division whereby southerners depending more on agriculture were more custom to the economics of France, whereas northerners tended more towards mercantile policies for controlling wealth. There are lessons to be learned from the positive and negatives of both policies for a more prosperous future of mankind in general.

It is now evident that we humans are our own worst enemy whereby political economics needs to evolve by more peaceful means involving more cooperation among ourselves. Although a threat of a nuclear holocaust has likely deterred the motive of wars between nations capable of using it, the threat of climate change could perhaps further provide more incentive for a common purpose that could, in turn, promote world peace. There is still a need for a fairer distribution of economic wealth. More prosperity for us all is most likely a requisite for a true world peace and tranquility.

3
POLITICAL ECONOMIC HISTORY OF EUROPE

A social aspect of economic trade could have begun in Anatolia as early as 12,000 BC, as from hunters seeking food from farmers and making stone age tools from a naturally occurring volcanic glass, obsidian. With development of agriculture, a more convenient means to barter for cattle and other commodities was grain because of it being more available and dependable. However, it required an intelligible means of record keeping. In Sameria, for instance, a token was impressed on a ball of clay, and it contained other tokens inside it. The outer token became a seal of identity, and it further ensured it had not been tampered with. This means of record keeping was popular up until the Bronze age when metal became the more convenient means of exchange.

Codes of Menes, who established the first dynasty of Egypt, stated that the values of gold and silver are two and a half parts of silver for every part of gold. Coinage eventually became used in China where copper coins were in use from 206 BC to AD 220 by the Han dynasty, and they have been reported to have been found in tombs that date as far back as the eleventh century BC. More location to the west was gold used as early as 643 BC in Lydia where smelting silver into gold produced gold coins by 560 BC. Gold subsequently became common as the most preferred means of exchange. However, it has not always been preferred. A fiat currency in the form of a tally stick was authorized by King Henry I, even for the use of paying taxes due to a gold shortage in England around AD 1100. Not until AD 1819 was a gold standard legalized in England, and the USA dollar was not redefined until AD 1900 to consist of twenty-five and four-fifths grains of gold, being one and three-fifths grams, although there had been an AD 1873 congressional act in the USA legislature that had omitted defining the dollar by weight of a silver dollar.

A form of money was printed on animal skin in China during the reign of Wu Ti just before the birth of Christ. Its use in China increased with the invention of the printing press. The Tang Dynasty (AD 618–907) printed around AD 800 what was called "flying money" that was easily lost to the wind from customers transporting goods by ships at sea. The printed cash tended to remain local where it could be reimbursed from the government as coin, salt or liquor.

Usage of paper money in China was discovered by Marco Polo in the thirteenth century. China improved its quality for a more convenient use of it by citizens in general. However, it was not officially issued by a government in Europe until AD 1601 by Sweden.

As for a means of regulating money, banking occurred in ancient Egypt and Mesopotamia with the storage of grain. The process evolved for people to be able to deposit anything from grain to a precious metal for sale or trade. However, although grain was valued for consumption, a metal soon became the preferred means of exchange. Grain becomes spoiled for one disadvantage, and its quality and taste are subjective to the preference of the consumer whereas metal is more durable and convenient for transport here and there. In particular, the rareness of gold with its durability and shiny attractiveness would become more favorable in manner consistent with supply and demand economics.

Economics as part of political policy was philosophized in early times. Plato, for instance, advocated a "credit theory of money" as a unit of credit or debt. Aristotle theorized property owners need to be allowed to attend to their own business in order to produce and exchange their common interests, and that monetary interest charged on a loan is unfair in that money itself has no real value other than as an instrument of exchange.

It is also evident that early banking had acquired an unfavorable reputation. Charging interest as usury was forbidden by the Catholic church and by Islam. However, exceptions occurred of the Knights Templar and the Jewish people of Israel. Accused of usury were members of the Knights Templar. They became exempt from taxation and from most local laws. Although they were forbidden to charge interest as a fee for holding money to safeguard, they charged rent as a loophole of the law.

The Knights Templar originated as military protectors of nobles who were often attacked and killed while on their pilgrimage to the Holy Land of Israel. The original Knights Templar consisted of only two brothers and five other relatives of Hugues de Payns. He was able to solicit permission from King Baldwin of Jerusalem for an Order that became headquartered over what is believed to have been Solomons' temple. As they became more popular, they were approved around AD 1129 by the Catholic church that granted them freedom to pass through borders.

Nobles graciously donated to the Knights Templar's cause because of its members having been granted charity status among countries of Europe. They were also exempt from taxation and local laws by an order of the pope. The latter condition was influenced by Saint Bernard of Clairvaux who was the nephew of Andre de Montbard. Bernard became Knights Templar chief during (AD 1154–1156).

The Knights Templar members as a charity organization were sworn to poverty, but they still accumulated great wealth and power. Their success came from recruits donating wealth for their cause, but the Knights Templar members eventually converted from military protectors to bankers by safekeeping gold in order to minimize the risk of travel. Wealthy nobles were given receipts for their gold so that they could redeem it from other Knights Templar members who located elsewhere.

Although the charging of interest was a forbidden act by order of the Catholic church, the Knights Templar members engaged in many transactions to collect rent instead of interest for held mortgages. However, their collection of revenue competed with the church. Their demise finally came in AD 1212 at the insistence of King Phillip of France confiscating their wealth in order to finance his war with England. They became outlaws in all western countries of Europe except Portugal that historically is the most profitable country whose bulk of population was to migrate to new places. About one-half of them relocated to Brazil.

Another exception of the law forbidding usury was granted to the Jews. According to interpretation of their scripture, it was forbidden for them to charge interest to other Jews, but they could charge it to non-Jews.

Jews living in Portugal, Spain and elsewhere became early bankers to fulfill a need caused by the religious restrictions that had been placed on Christians. In AD 1396, Jews were permitted banking practice in Florence, which did not become part of Italy until AD 1861. By the bribing of Pope Martin V in 1428, they became official bankers in AD 1437.

A main reason Jews were accepted as bankers is that they had been granted less rights and were thus believed to be easier to control. They had been relegated to ghetto status whereby they could be used as middlemen. The Germanic name Stein became required as part of their surnames to single them out from normal citizenship whereby they could loan and collect debt for the so-called European nobles, and they profited just the same to gain favor of rich merchants.

Not until the sixteenth century, when Protestantism became influential, after Martin Luther led his revolt against the Catholic Church in contesting such assertion that God's forgiveness can be bought in order not to be hell-bound, was banking officially accepted as a legitimate profession of the general population.

The economics of the time was also conditional to slavery. Expansion of colonies in the new world provided more means of obtaining economic wealth even though competition for such wealth increased along with war.

Harvest of ancient Roman grapes and olives had developed into large estates that provided a source of trade, but Rome resorted to the conquest of Egypt, Sicily and Tunisia when import of grain became less obtainable. Along with such conquest was the import of slaves for them to increase agricultural yield. In this tradition, France, Spain and Portugal also developed whereas England became more dependent on their merchants trading of manufactured products from natural resources.

Spain led the way across seas, but Fance and England became challengers to the stronghold on trade in the sixteenth century.

Queen Elizabeth of England warned that importing more goods for gold and silver than exporting it would lead to poverty of its nation while enriching foreigners. Political writers were encouraged to propagandize a policy now referred to as mercantilism. It generally included high tariffs, colonization, restricting the export of gold and silver by the colonies, and forbidding colonies to trade with the use of foreign ships. Low labor wage was also encouraged for the sake of profiting from forcign trade.

Labor itself was a primary means of obtaining economic wealth. An import of natural resources could be manufactured into finished product to be exported as trade for more gold and silver. This accumulation of gold and silver was considered ideal to compensate for increase in population and the funding of a military along with more industrial development.

Mercantilism was mainly about collecting gold and silver for national wealth. It required a large fleet for protection against pirates, and its effect coincided with a vigorous competition for economic wealth among nations that further led to more conflict and war between them. It also led to revolt from colonies opposing harsh restrictions imposed on them.

In contrast to mercantilism was an economics developed in France during the eighteenth century with agriculture as its basic wealth instead of gold. An agricultural base of wealth is reasonable in that food is essential to life. An abundance of it by means of farming fertile land had previously enabled the rise of our modern-day civilization.

Even though gold is more convenient for trade in that it is more long lasting than food, it is still non-essential for life itself. In order to survive the long journey through a desert, a canteen of water is worth more than a ton of gold. Although a means of exchange is still needed for a more general free enterprise system, it is only the acceptability of gold and silver that renders them useful for trade. Egypt once used stored grain as a means of exchange. American Indians and colonial settlers traded with the use of beaver fur, fish, corn and wampum (beads of shell).

In contrast to mercantilism was physiocracy. Its members advocated income from trade needs to be circular with the production of agriculture as its base value instead of merely accumulating gold and silver to finance the state of its imperial superiority. For this circular flow of money, laissez faire economics was proposed whereby minimal intervention of government allows freedom of interaction between economic participants with no need of tariffs. The funding of government only needed to be implemented by a single tax on the income of land owners. The tax was believed to provide the owners with the incentive needed for them to produce food to sell and be able to pay tax. This movement merely paved a way for an enterprise system to be free from governmental intervention.

A more general form of free enterprise developed in England whereby the import of natural resources had been considered needed for creation of manufactured goods by manual labor to export for more wealth. Because the more general form of free enterprise included all products as economic wealth apart from mere agriculture as principal wealth, it became a more general form of laissez faire economics.

The transition from mercantilism to laissez faire was a step-by-step process by such contributors as John Locke, Charles Davenant, Dudley North, David Hume, David Ricardo and Adam Smith. John Locke (1632-1704) of England agreed with a supply and demand theory of price and value, and supported individual property rights, but he also agreed with the mercantile policy of obtaining a favorable balance of trade as a competitive means of increasing wealth. Charles Davenant (1656-1714) published an essay on trade that seemingly understood merits of competition and consumer demand, and it noted that a favorable balance of exports could finance war. On the other hand, a disagreement of policy was offered by Dubley North (1641-1691) arguing that free trade promotes wealth for both sides in allowing a division of labor as specialization. David Hume (1711-1776) pointed out that imports of gold and silver from exports increases money supply and inflates price of commodities for it to render exports more expensive for other nations to purchase, thus preventing a restoration in balance of trade. To the contrary, a principle that is now referred to as comparative advantage was proposed by David Ricardo (1772-1823) whereby free trade can benefit both sides if each nation has a more efficient means of producing their own products to export.

Bernard de Mandeville developed a poetic satire that he first published in 1705. It became known as The Fable of the Bees. Honeybees robbing flowers of their pollen and nectar support the hive in a social manner. Their pollination is essential for plants to bear fruit, but an emotional connotation for poetic drama referred to this act as individual vice. It generated criticism along with the popularization of the theme that vice is individual action resulting in economic prosperity. It became interpreted as an "invisible hand" that unknowingly benefits the economy, and it was a phrase Adam Smith (1723-1790) used in the religious context of a godlike intent of opposing vice to prevail of individual action.

Smith acknowledged greed could have negative effects on the general welfare of society. However, resulting negative consequences could also be an integral part of the nature of laissez faire economics. A particular person who smokes cigarettes as part of an unhealthy diet is supportive to the employment of doctors and so forth for distribution of wealth and a prosperous economy of ample opportunity to succeed in life. In contrast, a person who eats healthy and exercises, and rides a bicycle instead of relying on an automobile for daily travel, contributes less to the economy and more to the self with less chance of environmental pollution. With more emphasis on economic wealth, there is a general trend of merchants to welcome people having more money to spend on merchandise.

Wealth becomes status. The person with the more expensive watch is viewed as a more successful individual. Having a greener lawn than the neighbor's is desirable. Economic wealth thus tends to be in the eye of the beholder. However, such social wealth as healthier climate to live in can also be a result of increasing wealth of the overall economy.

James Steuart Denham (1713-1789) published a comprehensive work in 1768 defending principles of mercantilism with the title An Inquiry into the Principles of Political Economy. It was countered by his fellow Scottish writer Adam Smith's publication of Wealth of Nations in 1776, which was the same year the United States of America set forth its Declaration of Independence from England. Smith's book is considered by most economic historians as most influential in modern economics.

Smith classified economics as a political inquiry into the nature of what determines the wealth of a nation's economy to provide revenue for public service. Does this classification indicate financing government is needed to determine wealth of its people to some extent? It could be interpreted as such by some of us, but Smith further advocated the concept of an invisible hand whereby a minimum amount of government allows innovation of individuals to have positive effect on the economy as a whole. However, whatever constitutes the minimum amount of government is somewhat controversial. Some politicians argue government only needs to provide security to enforce law and order, and to protect the nation's border from invasion. Other politicians advocate government has a vital role in determining such social aspects of the economy as social security and environmental concerns.

Labor had generally been viewed, even by Adam Smith, as the means of creating wealth. For a competitive advantage, a means to minimize labor cost was preferred whether it involved the use of such animals as an ox for plowing fields, slave labor, or taking advantage of competitive conditions of poor people seeking employment. Adam Smith further warned that corporations might take advantage of the poor by means of monopolization. Discontent was also noted by Marx and Engels of their Communist Manifesto as unfair distribution of wealth.

(Supposedly, monopolies and oligopolies are prevented from occurring by government, but the use of monetary wealth can also influence government officials.)

Although labor has and still does create wealth, it is not necessary that it itself is the controlling factor. Such energies as petroleum and electricity either help produce more product or decrease the need of manual labor. If computerized robots replace the need of human labor without additional product, then the controlling factor of wealth becomes ownership rather than labor, as for the rich to become richer among an overall poorer population in general.

Ownership is further influential of economic wealth in that owners of property have more credit by means of their property being usable as collateral. Credit becomes money. By ownership of more money, as to lend for profit, money is a means to acquire more of it (although not without risk). The competition for wealth inspires innovation for more products. However, if one competitor of free enterprise wins out, then the free enterprise system is won over by monopolization of money supply.

The means of monopolization was somewhat different in the past than what it presently is. As in the past, mercantile hording of gold or storing paper money underneath a mattress could have resulted in deflating prices of products to increase the economic value of gold. As in the present, inflation versus deflation is more influential on who controls the economy. Inflation regarding a monetary increase in wages and a fixed loan rate tends to either balance out or benefit some of us more than others. Paying back a loan of a previous date has become relatively less costly whereas new borrowers with the same monetary income have relatively more cost of purchase.

A better system of balance is thus preferable by some of us. Money earns money by some risk, but economic wealth should be a measure of product instead of money.

4
DEMOCRATIC REPUBLIC OF AMERICA

An influential factor of the American Revolution from English rule was interpretation of republicanism for the formation of government. Both Plato and Aristotle independently philosophized that democracy, aristocracy and monarchy combine to form a republic. Later ideas stressed the duty to enforce law of the land by means of liberty overcoming the corruption of government. England had become viewed corrupt as such by colonists. However, during the American Revolution itself, Continental Congress initially had no means of unifying the colonies. Because they officially were different established states independent of each other, they had no authority to tax or regulate trade. Payment to soldiers was thus dependent on each state to authorize its contribution. An urging for a central bank for the financing of military and other needs of government was later included in a newly formed constitution whereby the Republic formed was contained with a President, Court, Congress, and Senate. Inclusion of the Senate was a compromise whereby a number of Congress representatives are according to the overall population of every state whereas each state has a number of representatives for the Senate according to their separate populations.

Virtues of republicanism were recognized within the colonies in a manner that rule for and by the people were favored. Republicanism, democracy and liberalism were thus uniquely intertwined in a popular way that could have enabled Thomas Jefferson to succeed George Washington as President, with members of a Democratic-Republican party popular in name that had been founded by James Madison and Jefferson. However, the authoritative nature of the new nation as a republic remained controversial. Thomas Jefferson, Thomas Paine and Benjamin Franklin asserted representative democracy as a preferred element essential to republicanism, but John Adams and Alexander Hamilton preferred more governmental control by leaders more knowledgeable of government instead of the common people with less understanding of it.

Contributing factors for unionism began farther back in history. In 1664, the British navy invaded New Amsterdam, which later became renamed New York City, and applied the mercantilism policy of enriching itself at the expense of colonialism. As England declined to furnish it colonies with coinage, and even forbit them from minting their own coins, colonies were dependent on barbaric methods to barter for commodities and services. Their exports were accepted by English merchants, but they received goods and services as trade without exchange of gold. A method of trade among themselves thus resorted to such items as tobacco and rice as money in southern colonies. Included as various forms of money were animal skins, livestock and so forth, but their impermanent nature and variance in value were far less convenient than gold.

Dutchmen trading with Indians in the area of New York City introduced, in 1627, wampum (shell beads) to New England inhabitants as a method of trade. Ten years later, wampum became legal gender for paying taxes in Massachusetts. However, it became illegal twenty-four years later. The likely cause of its illegalization is that it was too fragile for practicality, and its productive potential could have been too uncontrollable as well as were amounts of gold and silver in later years.

In 1662, there had been an attempt to establish a mint in the Massachusetts Bay colony in Boston. It failed mainly because of its simple design being easily counterfeited. In 1684, attempts to mint coin were further thwarted with the closure of the mint by order of King Charles II of England. He revoked a fifty-five-year-old charter of self-management. Colony members consisted mostly of Puritans detested by the royal order for their attempt to purify the Catholic church. Charles II accused them of insubordination.

Colonists were still dependent on a currency for community services. A likely candidate available to them was paper money. Paper at the time was not as durable back then, but it could have been a more convenient means of exchange for circumstances at hand. In 1690, the Massachusetts Bay colony thus printed the first paper money in North America. The practice was soon followed by other colonies. However, if paper money was not backed by either gold or silver, it would be worthless against the purchase of European commodities. Paper money thus became notes of credit with the condition they were redeemable for gold and silver.
However, even though owned land could have also been considered as collateral for paper credit, the notes rapidly depreciated in value because of not enough gold and silver available for redemption.

Land banks were created in the following century for the transactions of mortgages, some of which were by government agencies. A few commercial banks briefly existed. Some of them were fraudulent; others were closed for being in violation of English law, such as was one established in Philadelphia by Thomas Willing and Rober Morris.

Such circumstance as war created another need for paper money. So-called continentals were issued by the Continental Congress between 1775 and 1779 in order to help finance the Revolutionary War of Independence from 1775 to 1783. As a means of credit, a continental dollar equated with the Spanish dollar, but too many continentals became issued than could be redeemed for gold and silver, and they were decreased ninety-nine percent in value by 1779. The slogan "not worth a continental" persisted even after the colonies became victorious, whereby Continental Congress enacted in 1786 a constitutional law that forbid any state or federal chartered bank to issue paper money.

The constitution did allow borrowing of money. For purchase of such needs as guns and bullets, the war effort depended on financial support of gold and silver. Large sums of money were mostly borrowed from the French government, Dutch bankers and wealthy merchants located within the colonies.

Merchants opposing English policy aided the revolt. Robert Morris Jr. was a particular merchant in the Philadelphia Bay colony. As part owner of a shipping and trade company having international connections, he used it to spy on the movement of British troops. His firm helped sell spoils of war obtained from English ships by privateers. His own navy was eventually sacrificed for the cause. In addition, he personally donated ten thousand English pounds to continental troops under the command of General Washington, and he funded more than half the cost of bullets and other government expenses by way of "Morris Notes" of his own funds. However, he later invested his remaining fortune in land. He went bankrupt in 1798 after the bank of England suspended specie payments in 1797, and he served time in debtor's prison until being freed in 1801 after the passage of a bankruptcy act.

A close associate to Robert Morris was Alexander Hamilton who was an early volunteer in the revolt against English rule. While in New York, Hamilton joined a New York volunteer unit, received the rank of Lieutenant and was later elected captain. He became General Washington's top staff aide with the rank of lieutenant colonial. He requested an active role in the field of battle. Washington was reluctant to sacrifice the communication talent of his top aide but eventually consented, giving Hamilton the command of an infantry battalion from New York that forced a critical surrender of the British army at Yorktown, Virginia. President Washington then appointed Hamilton on September 11, 1789 as the first Secretary of Treasury.

Although the colonies revolted against English rule, their merchants did not oppose the English banking system. They were practitioners of it in need of a system of credit whereby those with wealth could invest in those unable to create wealth because of not having enough of it at hand. Up until the year 1781 the local means of credit relied on such individual transactions as that of an owner of land using it as collateral to obtain a loan from an individual or company. Land owners included government as well as individuals.

Philadelphia merchants had established the Bank of Pennsylvania in the year 1780 to help finance the war, but it was not a real bank in the ordinary sense. It resulted in rampant inflation partly due to an issue of $240 million credit in banknotes by the Continental Congress that was to be redeemed for gold and/or silver, and partly because the states charging their own banknotes were counterfeit according to British rule. Such factors resulted in not enough silver and gold available for all individuals to redeem notes on demand. The states and federal government thus remained in debt after the war. However, the vast amount of open land in North America was recognized as an attractive investment opportunity. Robert Morris, for instance, was able to obtain a sizable loan from a France bank to invest in establishing the Bank of North America.

In the year 1770, Hamilton proposed to the Superintendent of France, Robert Morris, the need for a national bank to help finance the war. Morris agreed by submitting to the Confederation of Congress a request to officially charter the bank. The request was granted in 1791 for it to become the Bank of North America.

It was the first privately owned bank of the United States, and it was partly financed by his ability of obtaining a loan from France. However, the debt kept increasing.

In response to the Bank of Pennsylvania's failed attempt to finance the war, Morris did attempt to solidify the Bank of North America with specie. However, the bank was accused of being a monopoly. The monopolization practice of the bank was actually endorsed by its backers as necessary in order to survive during the wartime, but wartime privilege allowed discrimination of loaning practice to whomever board members of the bank preferred to loan to. More banks became more desirable for fair play.

The first constitution of the United States was an agreement called the Articles of Confederation and Perpetual Union. It was ratified in the year 1781, and it forbade taxation by the federal government that could then only borrow money from the states. Congress also lacked authority to regulate the trade of states between either themselves or with foreign countries. States of the Union thus had independent control of their own trade policies. However, when the federal government failed to obtain its needs from states, this original constitution was replaced with a new one ratified in the year 1789 whereby the Secretary of Finance, Alexander Hamilton, founded a national banking system similar to one existing in England.

Hamilton studied such economic theory as authorized by David Recardo (1772-1823) advocating that government have a significant role in economic development. England had used public debt for building its military, not meaning the banking system was the cause of it being such a dominant force. The greed for more gold as economic wealth was more likely the contributing factor. With the unifying aspect of government in mind, Hamilton successfully proposed to Congress it charter a national bank similar to the Bank of England. The Bank of the United States was thus chartered in the year 1791 for a twenty-year period.

5
BANK AMERICA

A difference between the national bank of England and the one in USA was only that shareholders of USA banks had more votes for more shareholders whereas the one of England allowed only one vote for each shareholder. Another difference was that the USA bank charter restricted the amount of loans offered according to amount of gold and silver in reserve whereas England's charter ban placed no such restriction. Moreover, whereas the USA government was a shareholder with twenty percent ownership, the bank of England was totally privately owned.

Critics of Hamilton have labeled him a mercantile in association with Ricardo. Adam Smith had also suggested the USA should remain an agrarian society instead of attempting to become an industrial one of manufacturing products. However, Hamilton was more in tune as a businessman in realizing the critical need for financial institutions being able to pay debt of financing. He had, in AD 1784, previously organized the bank of New York.

The accusation that Hamilton was a mercantile has been rejected by some of his supporters claiming he simply realized free enterprise also requires protection and support of government. There was no appreciable amount of national debt among states during his time as Secretary of Treasury, and he realized a consolidation of state debts into a national one could help unify the states in support of a central government. To pay national debt, he proposed the creation of a national central bank for establishing the means for credit and investment to be financed by a tariff on imports, taxing distilled liquor, and by selling bank shares to citizens and foreigners for the promotion of such infrastructure of roads for the growth of an industrial economy as well as financing of military and government.

Such proposal can be categorized as selling of government stock. It was considered unique inasmuch as there is no redemption required of its sell. If the stock's company fails to succeed, the investor suffers the loss. For it to become an attractive investment, taxation provides a means of securing it for future dividends. Investors of it would also be more inclined to support a financed institution of such government of the people having a more general inclination of support.

The proposal was difficult to accept particularly to the southern states that were more generally comprised of conservative members of the Republic party, which included President George Washington. Secretary of State Thomas Jefferson favored the agrarian nature of wealth, feared a national bank would become an unfair monopoly in competition with state banks, and he doubted the constitutional legality of the national bank. James Madison, who was Representative House member of Virginia, also objected to the twenty-year charter of the bank as too long of a temporary operation. Nonetheless, the bill for authorization passed both in the House and Senate, and Hamilton persuaded President Washington to sign it into law. The First Bank of the United States was chartered for a period of twenty years from December 12, 1791 to March 3, 1811. It was headquartered in Philadelphia where it branched out into other major cities from New York to New Orleans.

The maximum capital of the bank was set at ten million dollars, and it was financed as a stock of paper notes to be distributed as currency. The government was the major stock holder at two million dollars. It thus shared in the profits, but it had no direct control of its operations. The national bank also competed with state banks, but the government attempted to control availability of credit by the issue of notes by state banks for the purpose of national security.

The first few years of the charter were unstable. Government scripts were initially sold as down payments for shares of the Bank. A competition for the scripts resulted in up-and-down periods of investments. However, the printing of notes was backed-up with the minting of coins, and the situation stabilized after a few years. Perhaps a discovery in North Carolina aided the cause. The USA mint only reported, in year 1793, that gold was being produced in a state. A large nugget was found in year 1799 by a young man, Conrad Reed, that became used as a doorstep for three years until a jeweler revealed to the family it was gold.

All currency was foreign from a circulation of coins minted in Mexico and Europe up until the national bank was established. An official mint by Act of Congress enacted in 1792 became operational in 1793. Most coins contained a percentage of silver. A nickel, for instance, was half the silver of a dime. Some coins also contained gold for a monetary rage in value from two dollars and fifty cents to twenty dollars.

The official value of a one-dollar federal banknote was about three-hundred and one-fourth grains (two-hundred-fourteen and fifty-six one thousand grams) of silver, but both silver and gold would vary according to its supply and demand for various products.

The first twenty-year charter seemed successful, but its renewal rested on Vice President Clinton for his tie breaking vote against renewal. In the following year, the USA got into a military conflict with England for two and a half years that resulted in a period of inflation. Not until 1816 did President Madison sign into law the second twenty-year charter, but its renewal in 1836 was vetoed by President Jackson favoring presidential authority for unity of government, and he also regarded the Central Bank as a threat to monopolize the banking rights of the states.

About seventy percent of the Federal Bank stock was foreign owned in 1811, thus aiding the depletion of its specie reserves of gold and silver. Moreover, agriculturists in the southern states complained of the bank providing an unfair advantage in favoring the development of industry over agriculture. In turn, industrialists located mostly in norther states complained the southerners had an unfair advantage with the use of slavery. The debate would eventually result in the Civil War from 1861 to 1865.

A favorable argument for renewing the charter for a central bank was that about five million dollars in paper currency accounted for about twenty percent of the money supply in circulation. However, bank notes issued by the National Bank were not discounted. Revenue by the federal government was obtained by such other means as taxation whereas profit of state banks was dependent on a discount whereby redemption of notes could be anywhere from zero to one-hundred percent less than their initial value. The National Bank thus had a competitive advantage in offering full redemption of all its notes to be representative of a currency of constant value.

After refusal to renew the National Bank charger, it resulted in a seven hundred and twelve increase in the number of state banks.

After a war with England occurring in 1812, industrialists in northern states began lobbying for tariffs on imports. Tariffs partly neutralized wealth obtained of southern states from the export of such agricultural products as cotton that were partly produced by means of slave labor.
They rendered imports more expensive for the benefit of financing industrial investment of the federal government. When President John Quincy Adams signed a Tariff of 1828 into law, the state of South Carolina threatened to secede from the Union. President Andrew Jackson, who was inaugurated in 1829, was a Jeffersonian in favor of such state freedoms as banking, but he also considered a strong Union as beneficial to the security of its people. He thus countered the South Carolina rebellion with a show of military force. A compromise was reached whereby the duty fee on Tariffs was lowered.

Still favoring free state banking, Jackson vetoed, in 1832, the renewal of the National Bank charter due in 1836. He further used an executive order, in 1833, to not fund the National Bank, and he used another executive order, in 1836, that required the purchase of government land be paid only by either gold or silver coins. Jackson, who owned hundreds of slaves, was a recognized hero of the war of 1812, and he favored unity of states without monopolization of federal government. He helped to form a democratic party whereby its members became referred to as Jacksonian democrats.

The national debt was completely paid off in 1835 for the first and only time in USA history. The economy was prospering when Jackson became President, mainly due to exports from farming, tariffs and the sale of public lands obtained from territorial expansion. Exports further provided an abundance of silver from China and Mexico. However, such a means of prosperity resulted in inflation for a panic to occur in 1937 that resulted in a seven-year recession.

The recession partly related to trade with England. A sharp decline of England's gold reserve occurred due to more imports than exports resulting in less harvest of its wheat. A counter to the effect was to raise the interest rate to discourage borrowing that further decreased money circulation for less import purchase. Rise in interest rate resulted in less money circulation that tended to increase the need for credit while decreasing the ability to purchase products from either within or beyond its borders.

USA's and England's recessions interrelated. The yield from exports of cotton declined. Moreover, USA banks had relied on English bank loans to fund such projects as industrial expansion to the west. With a stiffer price of these loans, and with gold and silver as a stiffer requirement for the purchase of government land, the result was also less loans and less competition for the purchase of land, resulting in deflation of prices as well as bank failure, less production and higher unemployment.

A recovery from recession began after a couple years. Part of it is attributable to a liberal banking policy that had been initiated by Jackson. A free banking period was in effect from 1837 to 1862. States during this period had chartered banks without the oversight of federal regulation. Although banks were required to issue bank notes in lieu of silver and gold coins, such reserve requirements as interest rates for loans and deposits were determined according to particular state policies. For instance, a Michigan Act of 1837 allowed banks an automatic chartering with no need of consent from state legislature. As other states generally adopted similar policy, loans became more liberal along with less bank failures. About one-half of the failures occurred within five years mostly because of their inability to redeem their notes.

Gold was also discovered in 1848 in the hills of California that attracted a large increase in population of immigrants mostly from Asia and South America. More than twenty thousand of them came from China. However, very few prospectors became rich. Of positive effect, the increase in population countered the inflation factor of more gold. Business thus capitalized more by taking advantage of the increased population in catering to it in becoming a surer means of obtaining economic wealth.

Causal indications vary. Too lenient restrictions of state banks could attribute to their failure. Daniel Sanches attributed bank failures to an inadequate restriction of free banking whereby smaller banks were at a disadvantage. To charter a bank, states generally required a condition of collateral for notes of credit to be backed by specie of such securities as government bonds to refund the notes on demand. However, the actual value of the state bonds was subject to the stock market that differed from their required purchase price that maintained intact as their collateral requirement. When market value of bonds lowered along with runs on banks occurring to redeem notes of specie, smaller banks tended not to have the collateral needed for them to comply.

6
SLAVERY CONTROVERSY AND CIVIL WAR

An influential factor in the development of Colonial America was the mercantile policy of Europe along with slavery. As European nations competed for natural resources to develop trade for monetary wealth, as by exporting finished products for gold and silver, they resorted to low wage labor that trickled down to slavery. English law forbade the enslaving of Christians. Native American Indians were not easily controlled for them to be exported and sold as commodities. Imports from Africa by way of Spain, France and Portugal became slaves for the purpose of agrarian and mining production. Indentured servant, being indentured for reimbursing cost of transport to the new world, was another option. After serving their time, they could become free to acquire land and so forth. Even some Africans became free citizens after they were baptized. However, stringent rules along with high taxes that England imposed on its colonies contributed to revolts. A contributing factor for unification instead of revolt seemed to be a central banking system.

John Locke (AD 1632-1704) is considered by some historians as the founder of classical liberalism. He invested in a Royal African company for the trade of slaves and drafted constitutions for Carolina in establishing a feudal aristocracy allowing slave owners full mastery over their slaves. He believed atheism should not be tolerated. At that time, only slavery of other Christians was outlawed. His opposing aristocracy and slavery in his writings seems to have referred to the elite who, in some circumstances, were obligated to revolt against corruption. He also believed government should be divided into separate authorities.

All states except South Carolina outlawed importation of slaves in 1808. However, the invention of the cotton gin was instrumental in providing a lucrative cotton export from plantation owners in the southern states from which slave labor remained useful as a means of harvesting. Authorities in northern states countered with tariffs. Whereas they favored economic unity by means of the central banking system, southern state authorities favored independence of states.

While slave labor was favored in the southern states, manufacturing of product was the main objective of northern states. Slaves gave the southern states an advantage. A counter benefit for northern states was government tariffs imposed on imports countering tariffs from other nations that became as high as sixty-two percent in 1828. It resulted in relatively more expensive exports in comparison to those of other nations. As more expensive tariffs in contrast to free trade favored northern states, southern democrats became persuasive to a gradual lowering of price, but conflict remained regarding slavery. After the USA gained control over New Mexico in 1848, southern state authorities aimed at expanding slavery into the newly controlled lands of USA, and there was some contention of expanding its control to Cuba and into Central America as well.

This expansion of slavery was regarded as a disadvantage to the northern states. Compromise of an equal number of slave states to free states had previously been in effect from 1803 to 1854, but free states had outnumbered slave states. Southerners regarding this outnumbering as a threat to their use of slavery declared their independence from the Union. In response, authority of government became controversial regarding state and individual rights versus federal rights. Some merchants felt the need of a central bank for a stronger union; others feared the central bank could become a monopoly with an unfair advantage in competing against state-chartered banks. Moreover, there was controversy over whether states should have their own right to own, buy and sell slaves from which there became the Civil War. It began in 1861 and ended in 1865 with a military victory of the northern states for the abolition of slavery. However, neither northern nor southern states had been financially prepared for their way to victory.

The southern states typified a farming community whereas northern states were inclined to specialize in banking, manufacturing and such transportation as shipping. In order to finance the war, a source of revenue was required, but a domestic tax on citizens and local products was unpopular in both northern and southern states. However, northern states had an advantage of northerners favoring an import tax as a main source of government revenue, and they inclined to accept it as protection of their livelihood from less expensive imports of cheaper labor abroad.

Although the cheap labor of slaves receiving only food and shelter existed in the southern states, the outcome was vulnerable to the shipping control by northern states. When the southerners rebelled, northerners responded with a blockage of southern exports. It became a tactical success regarding its blockage of the lucrative source of southern revenue of export trade.

The tactic favored the north even though southern exports were interconnected with northern businesses as well as with European commerce. European manufacturing was able to obtain its imports from Egypt, India and Brazel for no need to become involved in internal conflict with American states. Although northern states had also been affected in regard to them benefiting from the shipping of southern exports, and even though northern banks held bonds as their securities that had been purchased by southern states, a shortage of wheat in England further provided northern investor an alternative. It was to invest in railroads of the Midwest for the transport of wheat and other commodities.

Economic circumstances thus favored northern states. However, initial conditions were still critically challenging. At the beginning of the war, northern states were direly in need of finance in order to pay their soldiers, purchase ammunition and so forth. The interest rate from state-chartered banks ranged from about twenty-four to thirty-six percent. It did not appear affordable at the time according to certain government officials. Change in the banking system was thus sought for the purpose of financing the war from which there was a security matter for the Federal Union to prevail against opposition to its existence.

The financial situation of government regarding its lack of funding was contrary to the economic needs of the time. The free banking period from 1837 to 1862 had experienced setbacks, but it was structurally coherent for the issue of credit for the general public. There was such cheating as counterfeiting and so forth, and a boom-and-bust period occurred here and there from time to time for various reasons. Some citizens suffered while others were able to take advantage of the situation, but the system was feasible with the overall ability of citizens to overcome such diversity with enough successful practice of accounting for their own individual needs.

State chartered banks during the free banking period were allowed by anyone meeting the requirements of the state charter. A strict requirement was a financial reserve to ensure bank notes could be redeemed for demand of either silver or gold. A penalty was accessed for failure of this requirement, but liability deposits for the issue of notes included government bonds that were issued either by a state or federal government. As long as they remained operative, they provided a reliable source of collateral unless the government itself became bankrupt, which the Federal Union nearly did in 1860. The success of both government and banking was thus still interdependent on each other during the free banking era.

The reason for this lack of government funding was another situation in itself. The California gold rush in the late 1840s had helped enable prosperity in the 1850s that included a construction of twenty thousand miles of railroad tracts by the sale of stocks, government bonds and land grants whereby the federal government even obtained a surplus. Lower tariff duties were thus enacted in 1857. However, a panic of 1857 followed a moderate recession to the economic boom. Part of its cause is attributable to the embezzlement of a branch of an Ohio Life Insurance and Trust company in New York City. Thirty thousand pounds of gold was sunk at sea by means of a hurricane. In response to its panic, President Buchanan hinted he might have to persuade Congress to pass a forfeit law canceling any bank charter suspending payment. He was then able to persuade bankers to hold one dollar in specie as security for every three dollars issued as paper credit. With the success of this persuasion, credit tightened to further result in reversing inflation to deflation. Foreclosures and bankruptcies of such companies as railroads and even banks soon occurred along with an increase in unemployment. Tax revenue, either tariff or domestic, was thus reduced.

Such events did not affect southern states other than rendering them a means of bargaining. President Buchanan being a Pennsylvanian democrat was inclined to compromise with the issue concerning tariffs for appeasement of both northern merchants and his southern democratic allies. However, USA tariffs that had been lowered in 1857 had become lower than those of most every other country. A fellow Pennsylvanian, Justin Smith Morrill, organized the Morrill Tariff of 1861 that Buchanan signed into law on March 2, 1861 just before Abraham Lincoln took office.
Seven southern states had already seceded from the union and elected Jefferson Davis as president of the Confederacy.

When Abraham Lincoln was elected President on November 6, 1860 as a member of the new Republican party that opposed slavery and had replaced the Whig party, South Carolina led the seven southern states to declare their secession from the Union. Both President Buchanan and President-elect Lincoln declared the secession illegal. When Lincoln took office, the USA Treasury had less than a half million dollars in specie, and it was millions of dollars in debt. Financing the Civil War was a difficult challenge. At that time, the constitutional law stipulated the Federal Government can only receive coins from banks or individuals, and banks were only willing to make loans to the government by charging interest between twenty-four to thirty-six percent. Rather than choosing from more than a thousand of different bank notes of countless banks charging such high interest, the USA government of the norther states chose to finance the war against the Confederate South by resorting to taxes on imports, individual income of citizens, property and so forth. Still, however, taxes in themselves were not an immediate solution due to a lack of specie that was required as a form of credit. There needed to be a form of credit to pay daily expenses at a future date.

Acts by congress permitted the government to both sell government bonds bearing interest and to issue demand notes redeemable in specie on demand that did not bear interest. However, demand notes were a difficult sell, and banks only purchased them at a discount to then loan them to the public for additional interest. Moreover, decrease in gold specie of both bank and government reserves occurred due to such factors as hoarding specie by the public, and the stock market of American securities was held in part by foreign investors draining specie from it. After December 31, 1861, both banks and the government Union terminated their redeeming of specie.

As a means to pay salaries to soldiers and other military expenses, Colonel Dick Taylor suggested to President Lincoln that patriotic soldiers would accept paper notes of credit not backed by specie requiring payback of immediate request. On the following February, Congress authorized the Legal Tender Act to issue one-hundred-fifty million dollars in legal tender notes for the replacement of the previous demand notes.

The new greenbacks known for green ink printed on their backsides were legal tender as fiat money except that holders of the notes could not use them for paying import duties, and the government could not use them to pay interest on its bonds. They were issued as a temporary wartime measure with the assumption that specie obtained by customs duties would eventually be available to be bought out of circulation. Because the treasury did not have enough specie to redeem demand notes, the USA Treasury was authorized by the Legal Tender Act to pay up to twenty percent interest for the redemption of the legal tender notes at a later date.

Rather than flood the economy with fiat currency, the legal tender notes helped in allowing citizens to use them for purchasing bonds. Secretary of the Treasury, Salmon P. Chase, hired Jay Cooke, a private owner of a banking house of the name Jay Cooke and Company, that was located in Philadelphia, to sell bonds for two years from October 1862. Their total value was estimated to be worth five hundred million dollars. Cooke was paid one-tenth of five percent for the first ten million dollars of bonds sold, and he was paid one-tenth of three-eighth percent thereafter. With the use of newspapers for advertising, citizens were persuaded that it was their patriotic duty to support their government. A low cost of bonds relative to the affordability of buyers had also affected the sale in providing the public with more opportunity to invest for six percent return of interest payable in gold after five years with full maturity of bond value in twenty years. The campaign was paid for as part of Cooke's commission, and it exceeded the five-hundred million dollars by eleven million that immediately became authorized by Congress.

Cooke was later authorized in 1865 to sell legal tender notes. He sold an amount of them worth over three-hundred million that enabled the government to supply union soldiers pay for their due wages. After the war, he participated in the establishment of a national banking system in helping to establish national banks at Washington DC and Philadelphia. His firm financed the construction of the Northern Pacific Railway in 1870.

Further remedies were needed to stabilize monetary supply. National bank acts were enacted in the years 1863 and 1864 with intent to establish a national banking system of national banks with a comptroller of the currency as part of the USA Treasury.
In 1865, for national currency to be in favor, non-national banks were required to pay a ten percent tax on their notes in order to withdraw them out of circulation. There was also an attempt of government to buy back the green backs with gold, but being popularly declared: "good as gold", they became preferable as the common means of circulation.

Although a national banking system was established similar to modern times, a particularly notable aspect critical to winning the war was bypassing banks in selling affordable bonds directly to the public in providing it with the opportunity to directly invest in its government. Especially essential to the potential of this investment is a government source of revenue. During and soon after Civil War times, the essential source of revenue equated to a tax and security of funding in relation to specie that differs from modern times whereby coin specie has been replaced with fiat currency of no gold or silver transaction. The fiat money of today is only worth what it can purchase. If there is product aplenty for a dollar, then a dollar is worth plenty amount of product. Money thus becomes useful as a convenient means of exchange of various products and services as a means of credit for investment. A particular money supply allows for more opportunistic means of creating economic wealth. It becomes dependent on the allocation of public debt more directly according to supply and demand economics instead of indirectly in relation to gold and silver.

7
CHANGE AND ADJUSTMENT ECONOMICS

A particular argument in favor of the gold standard is that its supply is determined by the finding of its users compared to a possible unlimited amount of printed money by the government. Although gold rushes have inflated economies, the periods of inflation have been relatively short and mild to allow natural adjustment by members of society affected by them. However, a counterargument is lack of gold in circulation, due to wealthier owners of it hoarding it, can disallow overall investment for production of goods and services. Bankruptcies are more likely to result from deflating the price of products whereby the hoarders tend to become richer on the average. However, with less production of goods and services, the hoarders themselves can also become less wealthy.

    Banking policy itself, either with or without the gold standard, can further be at odds with total economic adjustment. Inelastic currency after the Civil War resulted in such problems as unfavorable circumstances for farmers to finance their planting and harvesting of crops. At planting time, farmers needed loans in order to purchase seeds and equipment. After harvesting and selling their crops, they tended to deposit much of their profits in the national banking system. The money supply of banks fluctuated back and forth from high to low, and the Federal Reserve required banks to either sell bonds or stocks, or to call in loans. Without enough credit to plant and harvest, farmers became bankrupt in having to surrender their mortgages to banks. Financial crises occurred in the years 1873, 1884, 1893 and 1907 with the latter being the worst in USA before the Great Depression of the 1930s.

Developed nations in the latter half of the nineteenth century tended to comply with the gold standard as a common currency for a simpler means of comparing values of other currencies between nations. In 1873, the USA redefined its dollar in terms of gold instead of silver, and adopted the gold standard outright in 1900. A crisis occurring in 1907 further led to the federal reserve system according to the Reserve Act of 1913. It provided stringent rules whereby banks could borrow Federal Reserve notes to loan to customers.

The Federal Reserve was created to stabilize currency and gold values in compliance with an international gold standard, but such costs of World War I from 1914 to 1918 to fund military action persuaded many European nations to detach themselves from the gold standard. They gradually recommitted to it after the war during a time of prosperity in the USA until the Great Depression of the 1930s that prolonged longer than any other depression yet to occur.

As to why the Great Depression prolonged as long as it did, such monetarists as Milton Friedman and Anna J. Schwartz argued its main cause was a thirty-five percent monetary contraction resulting in deflation of prices, bankruptcies, unemployment and so on. Ben Bernanke, a Federal Reserve Chairman in 2002, agreed, and the British economist John Maynard Keynes had similarly argued recessions occur due to lack of public spending.

Differences between economists were of their solutions. Friedman and Schwartz argued for a gradually constant increase in the money supply to maintain a lower, more adjustable inflation rate whereas Keynes advocated assistance of government needs to be for better distribution of wealth, such as to be able to employ unemployed workers. Other means could be a policy of banks to impose a temporary redo of contracts resulting in too much debt. A postponement of mortgage payments during a recession to collect rent instead of payment on the principle, for instance, could prevent a great number of bankruptcies instead of banks having to foreclose on devalued property that is further vacated and devalued because of a lack of upkeep. Banks, potential buyers and renters could all benefit from such a change in banking policy if it is fairly implemented.

Whether Keynesian or Monetarist policies were or would have been either more or less applicable to the recovery is conditional to the situation at hand. An analysis here is only given for more understanding regarding circumstances relating to supply and demand economics and the economic policies in play after WWI and during the economic boom of the roaring twenties followed by the conditions of WWII.

It is not difficult for economists to examine abstract indications as to claim an initial recession would have been self-corrected in a fair amount of time, but the actual hardship experienced by countless victims of the depression was of economic tragedy to them. Such hardship included more than twenty thousand suicides, homeless citizens living in rusted out cars or on park benches while using discarded newspapers for blankets in order to endure the cold. Also included were children skipping school to help the family out with meager paying employment, and one and a half million wives strived to make ends meet with low paying employment after they were abandoned by jobless husbands. Moreover, more than four-hundred thousand farms became bankrupt with other farmer buying their corn and wheat and dumping milk on roads rather than to sell at lower prices to soup kitchens and long bread lines.

Latino citizens born in the USA were illegally deported along with minority workers being hired last and fired first, and there was a couple of WWI military veterans killed for protesting with many others citizens a veto by President Hoover of an early payment of a bonus promised according to a WWI Compensation Act of 1824. The promised payment was also vetoed by President Franklin Delano Roosevelt. Congress overcame the veto to finally grant a nine-year early payment in 1936.

Although not every American citizen experienced hardship, those that did were not simply lazy or incompetent, they were victims of the monetary circumstance of the time. One particular circumstance was how the gold standard influenced the economy after WWI. From WWI until the year 1929 the USA exports acquired from Europe provided a surplus of gold. By August of 1929 the Federal Bank's gold reserve nearly doubled what the Federal Reserve Act of 1913 required, and the USA accumulated about forty percent of the monetary gold of nations on the gold standard. It continued this hoarding trend into the depression whereby the USA and France accumulated about sixty percent of the monetary gold supply. However, they both endured more of the depression. Such nations as China and Spain that were not on the gold standard experienced less of it. England and Scandinavian nations that abandoned the gold standard sooner recovered sooner from it. The policy of the gold standard act regarding its implementation thus seems to have been flawed.

The founding of the Federal Reserve system in 1914 resulted from the Reserve Act of 1913. A main purpose of the system was to control money supply in circulation in order to prevent such banking panics as occurred in 1907. The primary means of control was in establishing an elastic currency in circulation that can be either increased or decreased to counter negative effects of inflation and deflation of the general economy. The Federal Reserve was established having authority to issue discounts to Federal Reserve banks for them to discount, in turn, other commercial banks and financial institutions.

The Federal Reserve was required to maintain at least a forty percent gold reserve for outstanding public loans. A Federal Reserve controller was authorized to control dire inflation effects whereby discounted interest rates were supposed to be increased to discourage public borrowing. With the higher interest rates paid to depositors of saving accounts, deposits would also compete against stock investments to also decrease the amount of money in circulation. Lowering of interest rates was then supposed to apply to adverse effects of deflation.

A criticism of the policy was that it could be too restrictive to properly work during some dire situations. It only had temporary loan control as a lender of last resort over member banks, but the number of state-chartered bank members of the federal system was only ten percent in December of 1929. The ninety percent of nonmember banks held about twenty-five percent of all deposits to all national and state-chartered banks. Nonmember banks and other investment institutions were also allowed to speculate in stocks.

An error of judgment occurred in August of 1929. The Federal Board responded in finally approving a request by the Federal Reserve bank of New York to raise interest rates. In response, foreign central banks raised their interest rates. Commercial banks of New York city became strained with rise in reserve requirement as the stock market capital transferred into banks. There was a stock market crash on October 29, 1929. The Federal Reserve then responded by lowering interest rates to successfully reverse the recession. This occurrence provided an indication of how banking policy could affect the world economy along with other failing events of whoever was at fault. However, other conditions emerging from the past were also to have negative effect.

While the USA maintained the gold standard while European nations departed from it during WWI, USA benefited from its financing European war needs and its recovery after the war. After a minor recession occurred in the early twenties, the roaring twenties emerged. Higher wages encouraged distribution of capital in promoting spending and investment. When government budget became a surplus, President Hoover proposed in the year 1930 a reduction of taxes by one percent, and subsequently proposed in 1931 a large tax increase in order to counter a budget deficit.

Although a middle class emerged in the 1920s, distribution of wealth was not proportionate. Average wages did not keep pace with profit, which resulted in less demand for products produced in 1929. In compliance with lower wages, farmers competed against each other, resulting in an increased supply and decreased price of harvest and livestock. As the price of farming equipment rose, farmers in debt struggled even more. A worldwide surplus of food seemed to emerge to challenge the price of farming products resulting from more efficient farming methods and new technology of modernized nations inclining to produce with more or less cost. Even though food could have been more plentiful, the greater competition to produce and sell at a lower price resulted in a more difficult situation for each individual farmer to cover the cost. Perhaps a counter to this deflationary trend could have been food stamps issued by government as a temporary means to counter deflation in support of the needy, but other deflationary tactics were employed instead.

Another notable factor contributing to the depression was a Dust Bowl of severe dust storms. Part of its cause was a severe drought caused by winds and farmers failing to protect their land. Destructive erosion of natural soil occurred in the years 1934, 1936 and 1940. Although farming production decreased for a relatively higher demand of food, it also resulted in higher prices of it along with less affordability.

Banks invested in stocks that declined in value. Some banks then were unable to operate in effective manner. The largest financial institution of the southern states, for instance, was a company named Caldwell providing banking, brokerage and insurance coverage. It lost a great amount of its capital reserve in stock investment. Following it, the Bank of New York ceased its operation. Credit became difficult to obtain. Hoarding money was more preferred.
Prices of commodities declined. Many companies, including banks, closed. The poor became poorer because of higher levels of unemployment.

There were thus lots of natural factors contributing to the Great Depression. Further detail is in reference to how recovery occurred.

Hoover became Presidente in March 1929. He proclaimed in his 1930 State of the Union Address, "prosperity cannot be restored by raids upon public treasury." His Union Address statement is consistent with his commitment to a balanced budget. He vetoed several bills intending to provide relief for Americans in need of it, but he also proposed such projects as construction of the Hoover Dam. In order to pay for them, he approved tax increases and signed into law a record tariff, being the Smoot-Hawley Tariff in name. A balanced budget was achieved in 1931 along with a plummeting economy of about a twenty-five percent unemployment rate. Although prices deflated, wages did not, likely due to support of unions among the work force. For companies to pay higher wages, they had to employ less workers.

In a limited way, Hoover initiated the New Deal that Franklin D. Roosevelt proposed after becoming President in 1933. What Hoover had included in the budget was additional revenue for national parks and forests along with the creation of the Veterans Administration for adding more veteran hospital facilities. He signed the Davis-Bacon Act mandating that all federal construction projects pay an above average union wage to all employees. He further pleaded to business leaders to pay fair wages for increasing spending and preserving the overall health of the economy.

The remedies were modest and restricted by law, leading to contraction of the money supply and a more lasting worst depression. By 1933, the unemployment rate had risen to about twenty-five percent in the industrial and mining regions of the economy. Farming income had become less than half of what it had been in 1929, and there was a closure of more than forty percent of eleven thousand national banks.

Bank runs were rapid. As Roosevelt took office in March of 1933, state governors had declared bank holidays in order to postpone bank-runs. The most immediate concern of the President was this banking crises. On March 5, he declared a four-day holiday to prevent further withdrawals and closures.

Congress, on March 9, 1933 passed an Emergency Banking Act allowing the President to intervene during banking crises in order for him to allow reorganization of banks, close insolvent ones, and to allow the twelve Federal Reserve banks to issue additional currency needed. With a plea by FDR for citizens to deposit their savings in banks, three-fourths of banks reopened by the end of the month. Bank security was further enhanced by a June 16 enactment of a Banking Act of 1933 for establishment of the Federal Deposit Insurance Corporation. In addition, a Securities Act of 1933 was enacted as a means to help prevent stock market crashes. On April 19, 1933, by executive order, FDR temporarily removed the USA from the gold standard.

An Emergency Relief Administration that Hoover had ceased in 1932 was revised as the Federal Emergency Relief Administration, and it eventually became the Works Progress Administration in 1935. It along with a Civilian Conservation Corps allowed federal loans to states and cities for employing unskilled workers in conservation and development of natural resources in rural lands owned by states, cities or the federal government. Development of a natural infrastructure was also included as part of the New Deal for building roads, hydroelectric dams and so forth. Farmers suffering from too low prices of harvest and livestock were provided relief by means of being paid for not producing. A Home Owner's Loan Act was also enacted. Congress amended Prohibition of Alcohol to allow brewing of a beer industry, and a National Recovery Act guaranteed workers the right to organize as a union to bargain for fair wages and working conditions. A national labor board was established by executive order along with the Civil Works Administration to provide work for about four million unemployed workers during the winter months of years 1933 and 1934. On June 28, 1934 a National Housing Act allowed the Housing Administration to insure loans for either repairing homes or constructing more of them. On August 14, 1935, FDR signed the Social Security Act that guaranteed pensions to retirees sixty-five years of age. It also provided financial aid to dependent children and the blind along with establishing unemployment insurance as well.

Some of these acts had both positive and negative effects. Labor unions can benefit workers with higher wages and better working conditions. They can also lead to unemployment and bankruptcy if companies cannot afford their cost. Paying to not produce food crops can benefit farmers by increasing prices, but it can also prevent the purchase of food by those in need of it.

Hoover and FDR both were proponents of a balanced budget. Some of the New Deal reforms were intended as temporary measures. Because of an improvement of the banking system, the early bonus payment bill to WWI veterans was vetoed, but the Congress, Senate and key advisers of the administration that FDR fortunately inherited were more willing to enact reform. Congress overrode the veto.

Those who favored the New Deal reforms became referred to as liberals. Those who opposed them became conservatives. The liberals had dominated, but conservatives became favored in mid elections between the years 1833 and 1835 due to such controversies regarding unionization.

The economy temporarily improved towards 1937, but the recession continued. Meanwhile, FDR concentrated on preparing for war. Congress had passed Neutrality Acts in the years 1935 and 1936 that prohibited exports for military war needs and extension of credit to any nation inclined to war, but FDR was more in tune with WWII initiated by Adolf Hitler of Germany.

Germany's economy, second only to USAs in 1924, had been devastated in 1918 due to WWI. By treaty, Germany was obligated to pay victims reparations for war damages. Because it was unable to compensate, France and Belgium invaded Germany in 1921 to strip it of its raw materials. During the year 1923, Germany experienced hyperinflation by printing fiat money in order to pay striking workers. However, Germany became extremely prosperous and peaceful from 1924 to 1928 due to gracious credit of the USA. However, gold reserves of the USA declined in 1929 along with requesting Germany to pay off its dept. Perhaps this policy reversal, in part, aided Hitler's decision of war.

During the years 1937 and 1938 the USA economy was in decline, but it stabilized in 1939 and began to soar in 1940 with a German invasion into France. The increased USA money supply was countered by investing in rearmament.

Lower priced bonds were sold that rendered more public investment. Taxes were increased, but mandatory rationing benefitted the overall economy regarding what the money helped produce.

A lend-lease program of the USA also supplied allied nations along with a French resistance force against Germany. Supplies included food, oil and other material needs. Subsequently, national leaders gathered in Bretton Woods, New Hampshire of the USA to establish, in 1945, a Bretton Woods international Monetary Fund policy. It required individual countries to maintain a one percent exchange rate variance of the gold standard in promoting monetary cooperation and financial stability to facilitate international trade, promote employment, sustain economic growth, and reduce poverty. A Marshall Plan was later implemented in the USA to help finance Europe's recovery. A foreign aid policy followed. USA charity dollars provided incentive for importing USA products that helped increase employment and positive distribution of wealth among USA citizens.

Give and receive was the outcome. In contrast, not having all that aid would likely have resulted in a grave outcome of economic disruption.

8
TRUE ECONOMICS AND REAL WEALTH

USA experienced budget deficits during World War II, but positive results occurred in the overall distribution of wealth. The rate of inflation after the war was modest for decades with low interest rates encouraging such investments in housing among a middle class enjoying the American dream. In the latter half of the century, distribution of wealth seemed to once again benefit wealthier citizens in manner of resulting in a fragile economy along with periodic recessions.

By 1960, USA held nineteen and two-fifths billion dollars in gold reserves that included one and three-fifths billion as an International Monetary Fund. Eighteen and seven-tenths billion of it covered transaction of foreign dollars, but not with positive results. As the USA economy prospered, Americans bought more imported goods. A balance of payment deficit then worried foreign governments that the USA would no longer back up paying in gold, and by 1970 the USA held fourteen and a half billion dollars of its gold reserve against its foreign dollar holdings of fifteen and seven-tenths billion. On August 15, 1971, by order of President Nixon, the gold ratio of the dollar was changed from thirty-five to thirty-eight dollars per ounce, and the Federal Reserve no longer was allowed to redeem dollars of gold. The USA further raised its standard gold value to forty-two dollars per ounce in 1973 and decoupled from the gold standard altogether in 1976. The monetary value of the dollar simply became whatever it was able to purchase.

Although gold can still be used to compare values of different currencies, it is not needed as such. Consider marbles instead represent various products. In accordance with domestic demand, if producers in the USA produce ten marbles at dollar cost to sell for ten dollars, whereas France produces ten marbles at a cost of ten francs to sell them for one-hundred francs, then ten francs equate to the value of a USA dollar. Moreover, if France doubles its printed amount of currency in circulation with no other changes regarding population and amount of produce, then twenty francs tends to become worth a USA dollar. The comparison is the same in relation to either marbles or gold. Thus, since the true value of gold depends on the available amount of product, actual wealth is product itself instead of gold or any other representative of exchange for products and services.

Another argument against the gold standard is that gold, as a particular representative of wealth, is more difficult to obtain along with being more rigid in adjusting to inflation and deflation. If, for instance, population and its productivity remain the same for both France and the USA, a fiat money standard allows nations more flexibility to adjust to their domestic situation than does a limited amount of gold reserve. However, criticism of a fiat money policy in place of the gold standard is that fiat money can more easily allow a nation to suddenly change the value of its monetary currency in a way it tends to alter true exchange values of imports and exports in its favor.

Similarly, a main criticism of the gold standard could be of it providing an international standard for trade that can also be an advantage of one nation over another because of there being more of its existence found within a nation that can take advantage of it, as even to hoard it for it to be of more demand. Gold itself could be more popularly considered as having more economic value than actual product merely due to its traditional value instead of its actual value.

Fiat money as credit can be a facilitator for economic wealth, its application is more complex. Along with the Federal Reserve needing to control the amount of money in circulation, as to prevent negative effects of inflation and deflation, there are stock market investments competing against government bonds contributing to bank interest rates and expenses of commodities. When interest rates become higher to counter inflation, investment in gold has been preferred as a better alternative. However, the real solution seems to be that of adjusting to change. Those of us who purchase a house at a low interest rate before its monetary value increases with inflation have a chance of selling it for more profit before higher interest rates discourage others of us to purchase it. True wealth being of commodities, it maintains with the ownership of durable commodities. However, if a house becomes infected with asbestos, its result could be of less value when sold, even at a higher price as only due according to inflation. Knowing how investment in products can properly be maintained is critical to success.

During and after a recession beginning in 2008, the Federal Reserve had been waiting for inflation to occur before increasing the prime interest rate. No such inflation occurred even though there was a substantial increase in national debt. An issue of concern became who or what was to blame. The general public itself had very little if any control of the matter except for whom they voted for political leadership.

What needs to occur is an even and fair distribution of wealth for ample opportunity for our success to experience the American dream. It could have occurred sooner with more government investment in infrastructure, such as had previously been done of railroads and is still being done of highways. Such investment, as had been done during the Great Depression, can reduce unemployment and create social wealth along with economic wealth. Such claim is further evident of how USA helped itself and other nations recover from the Great Depression.

Deflation after a period of inflation is generally considered a critical part of whatever causes an economic recession. For instance, the recession beginning in 2009 has been claimed to have been caused by a housing bubble along with a too lenient policy of bank lending. The too lenient lending policy consisted of insecure loans whereby a ratio of home buyer debt to available income gained fifty percent from 1990 before peaking in 2006, and becoming lower in 2007. In effect, the increase in bank interest rate along with a too lenient loaning policy led to bankruptcies of borrowers who could not afford paying back loans along with less bank income.

The fourth largest financial firm in the USA, Lehman Brothers, filed Chapter Eleven Bankruptcy Protection on September 15, 2009. It appears to have been the start of a worldwide trend of deflated pricing due to less credit available for sufficient circulation of money needed for the purchase of products.

Particular balance of consumable product and monetary circulation can possibly avoid a recession and promote prosperity instead. Possible result includes distinction between economic wealth and social wealth as each being parts of functional balance. Social wealth includes the quality of air we breathe having little, none or even negative economic value in relation to free enterprise. It is here proposed that investing in a healthy environment in some ways can contribute, as a positive part of social wealth, to the overall production of economic wealth. However, it can also be a negative contribution if not done in such proper manner exemplified by investment in the structure of the Grand Coulee dam in the state of Washington during the great depression. With citizens unable to invest for the creation of more wealth, the social policy of government can be a better alternative.

Climate change is of similar analysis. Carbon as part of food can be more easily digested if heated at relatively lower temperature. If heated at a higher temperature, it becomes more self-bonded to clog up parts of the human body. Also heated at a favorable temperature, carbon soil tends to be more nutritional. However, if heated at a higher temperature, it tends to becomes more explosive. Moreover, if heated to a much higher temperature, along with more pressure, diamonds become creatable, which can also become more explosive along with other results of such processes.

Similarly, a paper or glass cup full of water can be boiled in the hot coals of a campfire, but attempting to put out a grease fire on a stove with water can merely fuel it. Different results are thus dependent on the degree of temperature and pressure similar to wealth being circumstantial according to different situations.

What constitutes real wealth? Although it had been measured in the past according to a gold standard, its measure is actually in the eye of the beholder, being actual product instead of gold or some other kind of currency.

Some proponents of the gold standard have argued the principal cause of inflation is the liberal printing of fiat currency. A counter argument is hoarding of gold leads to deflation and the accumulation of wealth by its hoarders. With less gold currency in circulation, lower prices of goods and services occur from which the hoarders of gold have more purchasing ability. Furthermore, the greed for power that the hoarding of gold might allow might also have led to wars similar to pirates stealing products and currency at sea.

The deflation argument is not without precedence. As to why the Great Depression prolonged as long as it did in the 1940s, such monetarists as Milton Friedman and Anna J. Schwartz argued its main cause was a thirty-five percent monetary contraction resulting in deflated prices, bankruptcies, unemployment and so forth. Ben Bernanke, the Federal Reserve chairman beginning in 2002, agreed, and the British economist John Maynard Keynes had previously argued recessions occur due to less spending.

A primary difference between arguments is with regard to their solutions. Friedman and Schwartz argued gradual increase in money supply for gradual inflation can promote spending in a way of it resulting in more investment of commodities before increase in their prices, whereas Keynes advocated government should assist in attaining a healthy distribution of its wealth by employing those on involuntary unemployment. Such solutions have been politically claimed to be socialism. Although they are socialistic in part, they can benefit free enterprise instead of countering it.

Effects of inflation and deflation are according to supply and demand. A non-inflation-deflation economy can occur if supply and demand maintain a particular balance. If there is an increase in population for more demand of products, then more production can satisfy the need for more purchases. Although the same amount of currency for the larger population indicates less money spent per person, it need not be in relation to money being merely credit. As long as more producers are needed for more production, then rise in the national debt ceiling is all that is needed. It can be invested in way of reducing unemployment that, in turn, creates more product.

Slight inflation could benefit in the sense of it providing incentive to spend in order to motivate more production along with maintaining balance of wealth. However, its outcome depends on both government investment and the ability of citizens of free enterprise. It can be argued that we who save more instead of living on the edge, as being more subject to debt, have more of a cushion to survive changing circumstances that result in bankruptcy. Being less able to afford both a new home and a new car is riskier if health becomes another factor for not being able to pay off debt. Saving by having less debt not only prepares for the future, it provides opportunity to invest in something later on of more promising investment of less risk. A house owner successfully renting and purchasing more property to rent could become wealthier whereas another property owner tending to spend more percentage of income is less likely to succeed. However, house values can also decrease by either lack of upkeep, as by allowing asbestos infection to occur, or destruction by fire or hazardous weather conditions. Insurance could thus be beneficial for having more positive future outcomes.

Individual decisions by members of the general public are thus essential to obtaining true wealth as well as is the application of government policy. Within a democracy of free enterprise, citizens need to become more aware of actual truth instead of just being influenced by a political blame-game. One elected President could inherit a recession for current blame instead of a pandemic while another could inherit a recovery from a present recession.

Generally, countering both inflation and deflation requires respective decreases or increases of currency in circulation. It could result from either the Federal Treasury controlling the national debt ceiling or by more spending per person for more rapid exchange of the same amount of currency already in circulation.

Although it has been argued that hoarding of gold has led to deflation and accumulation of wealth by the hoarders, fiat currency is also hoarded by being deposited in savings accounts with little or no intent for present spending. Investing in stocks for future retirement income can similarly reduce the quantity of money supply in circulation depending on how the investment is eventually used. Its value needs to maintain with inflation, which government policy supports. However, results are complex. A healthier environment for longer living conditions could thus have a negative effect on retirement income if government is not willing to increase its capable amount of funding. The increase in retirement income along with inflation tends to maintain balance along with supply and demand.

When hoarding of money leads to recession there is an easing policy applied by the Federal Reserve for increasing the amount of money in circulation, which can more effectively be applied internationally with the use of fiat currency than by changing price according to a gold standard. There was an attempt to counter inflation by the Central Bank system selling such government securities as bonds at a lower interest rate, but the lowering eventually approached zero. Since banks also paid less interest on deposits by the general public, the near zero interest rates by both Federal Reserve and banks became countered by stock investment. As stocks became a more popular alternative from the time of recovery becoming positive, their values increased along with dividend income per stock that is granted voluntarily by heads of companies supposedly for the sake of more attractive stock investment.

Rigorous loaning restrictions can also be another factor contributing to deflation and a slower recovery from recession. Although interest rates are lowered to help recover from a recession, banks become less willing to loan. The unwillingness is not merely because a thirty-year low interest rate could result in loss of opportunity to earn from a higher future interest rate. Although banks need to loan for them to generate income and pay operating expenses, the unwillingness to loan is mainly because of the stricter loaning conditions being of more risk during a period of recession because of borrowers tending to be more unable to pay back bank loans. Bankruptcies tend to occur instead.

A wiser alternative might be a temporary suspension of high mortgage payments in favor of affordable rent instead, as by extending the remaining contract to a future date. It could prevent the decline in values of non-occupied homes occurring because of their lack of upkeep. Extending the amount of time for payback could require an upkeep policy. Even though that in itself is only a possible alternative for bank owners to decide its feasibility, a temporary policy of government to assist home owners affected by the recession could be more beneficial in the long run as well, and the government does have determination of interest rates on government loans. Besides, wealthy owners of property are able to take advantage by cheaper purchase of homes of bankrupt owners.

What, then, are the best ways for government to help the nation to recover from recessions? It most likely depends on the situation at hand. The previous example of extending time of payment is in such a particular circumstance.

Another possible way is the Keynesian method of government increasing opportunity for employment. Generally, price of production is according to both cost and demand. If employment income becomes less, then demand becomes less as well unless an increase in population occurs as well. The latter also needs more sources of income.

Even though the general effect on the economy is mainly dependent on supply and demand conditions, government revenue by way of taxing wages and other earnings for government services can result in more flow of currency. However, if government services are considered more valuable than what is created in the public sector, then there is competition between wealth created by either social or individual free choice. Either one could be better than the other depending on particular circumstances.

It is arguable that a democratic role of government is not to compete with free enterprise, but in some respects the creation of social wealth is beneficial to economic wealth in general. If government invests in the infrastructure or roads and bridges, employment of government workers not only benefits the employees, it could benefit the overall economy of the immediate future and also prevent our grandchildren from being in debt because of too much repairs to overcome in future situations.

Investing in education can also be beneficial to the economy inasmuch as products could be more creatively produced. Electricity was discovered in the mid-nineteenth century. Its creative usefulness has been its supply merely resulting from flowing river water being controlled by dams. Social investment in the creation of dams resulted in more energy production for further creation of wealthier living conditions of the general public.

If additional non-competitive wealth is created along with an increase in the flow of money, it could simply result in additional distribution having ability to further provide incentive for producers to produce the same number of products that are of more demand. Increasing the national debt thus needs to be consistent with increasing more product of more demand for no non-adjustable inflation or deflation to occur.

If additional products and their demands counterbalance by additional money supply, then neither inflation nor deflation need occur. However, if government favors solar energy over carbon fuels, then it could counter free enterprise. However, it can also be argued that social wealth combined with individual wealth as total wealth can, in some ways, be more prosperous than that of merely producing individual wealth by means of free enterprise. The value of property, for instance, can be increased within a more favorable environment than that of climate change causing tremendous amounts of destruction.

A difference between social wealth and individual wealth is that the former can be environmental inasmuch as the air we breathe is essential to our well-being even though it has little if no positive economic value since its abundance is relatively free according to supply and demand. Although it can have negative economic value to companies required to either prevent or clean up their pollution of the atmosphere, it can have positive results as well.

If tax on air pollution is only used to clean it up, then social wealth created can be a non-competitive wealth in addition to individual wealth in the sense that both wealthy and poor citizens benefit from it. An issue of concern becomes whether polluters or the general public pay the expenses resulting from air pollution. Ideally, one way or the other would help maintain better distribution of the flow of money supply as credit for other purchases. To the contrary, however, even if tax on polluters helps persuade them not to pollute, too rapid a change in policy could affect producers of oil along with their stock owners.

Counter effects to overcome climate change thus tends to be, at the present, less popular. Still, the creation of social wealth can benefit the economy. More livable conditions can increase economic value of local property. As for government contribution, construction of highways and railroads have enabled an increase in traffic for the shipment of goods along with the ease of travel by citizens. Investing in the Gand Coulee dam in the state of Washington during the Great Depression assisted the growth of a farming community with water and electricity to spare. Investing in the infrastructure of roads, bridges and so forth could continue to benefit economic wealth. Otherwise, future cost of repair will be left as debt for our grandchildren to resolve. In this sense, more countering of present-day climate change could be beneficial to our grandchildren as well as a present benefit of employing the creative ability of those that have learned of more innovative technology to combat climate change. Social expense of government could thus be more effective than that of taxing the polluters.

A military for protection of the nation is an acceptable social part of government, and another national threat is that of climate change. Its debate began in the 1970s. During the last forty years the USA has experienced about three-hundred climate disasters with each exceeding a cost of more than a billion dollars. The problem of combating it is that there is no single solution as a particular method, either by an individual or even by a single nation. It requires a vast amount of effort by numerous people of all nations according to a Paris Climate Agreement requiring excessive carbon emissions contributing to it to become zero by the year 2050.

There are various solutions that can help. Conversion to electric vehicles is one that has potential for success depending on more creative use of wind and solar energy. Better insulation of homes and other buildings could lower cost against hotter summers and colder winters. An example of a possible remedy is blankets made in Taiwan containing bird feathers that are effective in maintaining the same temperature inside despite outside change in temperature. Natural gas is claimed to be the cleanest carbon fuel and its availability is plentiful in the northwestern part of the USA and elsewhere.

How should climate remedies compete against producers of carbon fuels?

Balance of wealth is needed to avoid monopolies and oligopolies, A game of billiards ends with a winner, but a balanced economy should not end with a single winner. In this sense, combating climate change could benefit both the poor and wealthy in way of obtaining better economic balance. With more drought and flooding for less food production, people tend to flee to more lucrative territories. If intruders at the border are hired as indentured servants to help counter climate change by increasing harvest and so forth, then it could become a plus instead of a negative. Another contributor of carbon dioxide in the atmosphere is people and animals breathing it out. Government financing of air purifiers could recycle carbon for better use of natural growth and benefit general health conditions as well as cleaner stores and homes for better living conditions. Such remedies here proposed are only a few examples of a multitude of possible remedies.

9
NATURAL CYCLES
OR
INDUSTRIAL CAUSES OF CLIMATE CHANGE

A previous belief of climatologists was that Earth's average yearly temperature had been constant for millions of years. It was challenged particularly by geophysicist and astronomer Milutin Milankovitch hypothesizing changes in Earth's revolution around its Sun results in more extensive temperature cycles than those merely of seasonal changes. Such change is still of natural cause, but there is now distinction between such national cause of climate change than such human cause by the use of too much fossil fuel. Their distinction needs clarification for more acceptable understanding the present cause of climate change.

Three different natural cycles of change occur according to the Milankovitch hypothesis of Eccentricity, Precession and Obliquity. Eccentricity is about a one-hundred thousand years change in Earth's orbit around its sun from being either more circular or more elliptical. Precession is about a twenty-six thousand years cycle in relation to how Earth's polar axis tilts towards its sun in relation to a particular distance of Earth's yearly cycle around it. Obliquity is about a forty-one-thousand-year cycle in relation to the amount of degree change occurs of Earth's orbital tilt towards its sun in manner of it also rotating.

What mainly influences Eccentricity is the larger planets Saturn and Jupiter having significant gravitational attraction on Earth. It had previously been reasoned that a constant yearly temperature results from all of Earth having the same average distance from the Sun per year. However, even though its yearly distance is nearly the same now than it was millions of years ago, the amount of time when Earth is either nearer to or father from the sun does change temporarily from the influence of other planets in the solar system. Gravity from farther distant planets from the Sun temporarily changes due to differences in gravitational attractions from Sun and planets varying according in time of year when sun orbits are either closer or father away from each other. However, such variance is relatively minute to balance out over time in comparison to more recent global warming slightly increasing over longer time.

Precession is in relation to how Earth's polar axis tilts toward the Sun in further relation to a particular distance of Earth's yearly cycle around it, as gravitationally influenced by both its moon and the Sun. It is about a twenty-six thousand yearly cycle compared to the one-hundred thousand yearly one. On January 4, 2001, Antarctica tilted towards the Sun at Earth's shortest distance from it to receive more sunlight during its summer than the Artic did during its winter. Likewise, the Artic received more sunlight during its summer than the Antarctica tilt during its winter, but less than the summer Antarctic tilt due to the Artic summer being of more distance from the Sun.

The approximate forty-one-thousand-year cycle of Obliquity also relates to the degree of Earth's tilt towards and away from the Sun, but its variance is according to wobbling of Earth's nearly perpendicular axis changing the time of year of a particular tilt towards the Sun.

On January 4, 2001 the Antarctic tilt towards the Sun occurred during Earth's shortest distance of the year. Antarctica thus received more sunlight during its summer than did the Artic during its summer. The Artic also received less sunlight during its winter than did Antarctica during its winter. Although the Arctic and Antarctica tilt away from the Sun for a colder winter and tilt towards the Sun for a warmer Summe, distances at particular times of the year gradually change. The summer solstice occurring in the Arctic six months later than in the Antarctica gradually changes within about a twenty-six-thousand-year cycle.

Notably, the last ice age that occurred about twenty-one thousand years ago had an average temperature of about eleven degrees Fahrenheit less than what it presently is. During the next five thousand years, the winter solstice should again be colder if the Precession cycle is to be solely the contributing factor. A speculative possibility is the Obliquity cycle being a slight change in the degree of axial tile could also change the amount of Eccentricity effect. However, there are other contributing factors to consider as well.

There are such other effects to consider for possible causes of climate change as volcanic eruptions and asteroid bombardment that are two different theoretical causes of dinosaur distinction occurring about sixty-five million years ago. The possibility of them occurring declines with those of greater magnitude, but effects of their past are nonetheless evident. As noted by Benjamin Franklin, winters in both Europe and the USA were abnormally colder after an eruption occurred on Iceland in 1782. During a period of about eight months of volcanic activity the atmosphere was filled with volcanic ash to interfere with the Sun's radiation. Climate was also cooler after an eruption of Mount Saint Helens in the state of Washington in 1980. Too much volcanic ash can thus cause cooling instead of warming by too much carbon dioxide in the atmosphere. However, that is only a temporary condition. More heat is eventually absorbed than lost over a longer period of time because of the greater amount of carbon dioxide remaining in the atmosphere to gradually absorb it.

Carbon is unique in having numerous differences in effects. For instance, water inside a paper cup can be boiled if placed inside the coals of a hot campfire, but water can also ignite more fire of something being cooked at a greater temperature, such as with grease. Paper is claimed to ignite at about one-thousand degrees Fahrenheit, which water in a cup prevents from occurring in contrast to grease more rapidly increasing in temperature by means of continual explosions being more numerous.

An eruption at El Chichon, Mexico occurred in 1982 having almost five times the cooling effect than the eruption at Mount Saint Helens. This latter eruption was of a smaller ash cloud containing more sulfuric acid particles remaining suspended in the atmosphere longer to either absorb or reflect sunlight back into outer space.

Earth itself has evolved from its beginning in manner of change occurring throughout the universe. Local changes can occur by means of astronomical influence. Difference in summer and winter temperature, for instance, can be more severe and volatile with various other effects. Glaciers of ice resulting from colder winters can reflect more sunlight back out into outer space whereas hotter summers of more surface water from melting of snow and ice absorb more heat at lower temperature.

Reflection of light energy as heat further relates to color. A white surface nearly reflects all imposing light whereas a black surface nearly absorbs all imposing light. Water, for instance, absorbs the penetration of light for possible internal observation, but ice having a white surface reflects most light. Although, the rigidity of ice can allow light momenta to pass on through for some of its energy to be stored somewhere else, there is less within being reflected back-and-forth.

There are also natural warming factors. Natural coal fires have existed for millennian, as in Wyoming and the western areas of North Dakota. What was once believed to be a volcano on the Australian Burning Mountain is now known to be a coal fire that has been burning for about six-thousand years. Natural coal fires result in the atmosphere absorbing carbon dioxide from them in what is now scientifically evident to be a warming factor.

Somewhat more speculative is the chemical complexity of how heat determines the nature of matter. As previously noted, water can absorb heat as demonstrated by boiling water in a paper cup placed in the hot coils of a campfire since it takes about a thousand degrees Fahrenheit for paper to ignite, but water can also fuel a hot grease fire instead of putting it out. Snow and ice of lower temperature can also be insulators preventing their containment from becoming even colder. Eskimos had lived inside igloos made of ice that kept their bodies from freezing from colder outside air.

Such other effects that sometimes occur are from the reduction of plant life. Less plant life can result in less absorption of carbon dioxide from the atmosphere for there to be a tendency of warmer weather. Colder water absorbing more carbon dioxide from the atmosphere allows more animal life to be born, as to produce, in turn, more carbon dioxide. More plant life and less animal life thus tend to cool Earth's atmosphere whereas less plant life and more animal life, including humans, tend to warm it. Although more animal and more plant life recycle, it is more recycling itself that increase the amount carbon dioxide in the atmosphere. Twice the amount of recycling result in twice the amount of carbon dioxide in the atmosphere. More absorption than emission is thus be needed to lower temperature of the atmosphere and prevent global warming.

The present concern of climatologists is a change to the carbon cycle. It is claimed that more carbon dioxide in the atmosphere results in the absorbing of more heat at a higher temperature of the same humidity from it containing more sunlight energy. In any case, the average temperature at the equator and the general atmosphere is claimed to be increasing instead of decreasing.

Global warming has resulted in more disastrous weather conditions. To understand how such results occur, consider why temperatures of islands near the equator remain mostly constant at about seventy degrees Fahrenheit throughout the year. It is partly because daytime and nighttime close to the equator remain nearly the same throughout the year and partly due to how heat is created and processed by water. Water can contain more heat at lower temperature. However, it can also expand in size. Since it consists of the smallest atom hydrogen, the expanded warmer air at the equator tends to rise instead to allow more absorbance of air farther away from the equator. The main result is circulation of wind. Moreover, such process can result in vulnerable hurricanes and flooding of composed air moving back and forth over water between the equator and opposite Earth poles.

Although both northern and southern parts of the hemisphere are becoming warmer, the overall rise in temperature consists of a more complex interaction. The cycle is just more energetic. The overall cause is a vacuum effect cycle of the warmer air being absorbed by the more extreme colder air from the North and South Poles whereby there is electrical attraction for condensation into rain clouds. Centers of attraction, referred to as eyes of the storm, are also present whereby they become surrounded by the swirling of hot humid air that is lighter and easier for them to swirl away from the equator towards the poles. With more heat from global warming, they become more volatile and/or larger for resulting in more destruction by means of stronger wind and flooding.

Climatologists now claim air is hotter due to excessive use of fossil fuel being released into the atmosphere. There is an equilibrium state of balance known as the carbon cycle. Carbon is needed for growth of food and other essentials. We breathe in air for combining its oxygen with carbon for the creation of energy. For the process to be continuance, we breathe out toxic carbon monoxide, which is toxic for breathing back inside except for it absorbing more oxygen from outside air to become carbon dioxide. The latter is less toxic to breathe, but it results in the atmosphere absorbing more radiant heat because of it having a greater molecular bondage to separate it, such that additional carbon in the atmosphere results in an average rise in temperature.

Carbon in the atmosphere also bonds with hydrogen from water molecules for a greater humidity potential absorbing even more heat and water at a lower temperature. Carbon is unique in that it can bond indefinitely with itself to become diamonds and so forth. Our lives along with plant life need carbon for food and other essentials. However, preferable balance of it needs to be maintained. If too much of the dormant state of carbon is mined for fuel, and deforestation occurs as well, then the state of the atmosphere increases to a toxic level of higher temperature.

Moreover, greater containment of water, as by oceans, becomes a carbon sink providing sea life with food, but too much carbon dioxide absorbed by water also becomes more acid for water to become toxic to life within the oceans, and for life outside the oceans because of acid water as rain being absorbed back into the atmosphere. Conditions are expected to become worse in the future. It is evident that remedies of climate change are needed to both adjust to and prevent hazardous conditions of climate change.

The composition of air itself is more complex. Its main components include nitrogen, argon, neon and helium as well as carbon and oxygen. Nitrogen, oxygen, argon are also considered as gases along with the formation of carbon dioxide and water. Water vapor is estimated to be about ninety-nine percent of air. Dry air mostly contains about seventy-eight percent nitrogen, twenty-one percent oxygen, slightly less than one percent agon, and one fourth of a percent carbon dioxide.

The normal amount of carbon dioxide in the dry atmosphere is harmlessly small, but it becomes more hazardous as a greenhouse gas if polluted to a higher amount. Excess of it in the atmosphere generally occurs from the usage of fossil fuels as gasoline. A natural means of reversal is plant life absorbing carbon by means of photosynthesis.

Carbon itself is unique inasmuch as its atomic structure is such that it can continue to combine with even more carbon along with other atomic elements. Similar to atmospheric interaction containing more light at higher temperature, plants at higher temperature can have more interaction potential to absorb carbon from the atmosphere. Water is inclusive to the process. The doubling of six carbon dioxide atoms transforms them into an atomic structure being of six carbon atoms, twelve hydrogen atoms and six double-oxygen atoms, plus a separate particle of six-double-oxygen atoms.

Since excess CO2 in the atmosphere mainly occurs from the usage of such fossil fuels as gasoline, more development of electric vehicles is a more feasible alternative. Another remedy could be the development of more advanced air purifiers. Large grocery stores, for instance, consume excessive amounts of toxic carbon monoxide from shoppers along with their consumption of toxic pollen released during flower growth. Some of us tend to be more faintish while shopping at such particular times of the seasons. Air purifiers is a possible solution in part, but at a cost to owners of the store unless there is a way to collect enough carbon that can be recycled for more production of products.

There is abundance of carbon usage. Most notable is it being a main source of diamond creation. Although such creation requires extreme pressure at high temperature, it is doable along with having further manufacturing usage. Since diamonds have longer lasting endurance, it allows them to become useful, longer lasting cutting tools with more grinding efficiency. Naturally existing as a poor conductor of electricity, they can be used as an insulator in similar manner of plant containment of particular atomic structures. They can also be used for creating pencils, more effective surgical instruments and so forth.

10
INVESTING FOR CLIMATE CHANGE SOLUTIONS

The main cause of climate change generally claimed by climatologists is excessive use of hydrocarbon fuels and deforestation. The former needs to be replaced by so-called green energy and the latter needs to be reversed. Proposed remedies include increase in plant life along with more use of such solar energy as sunlight and wind in place of carbon fuels.

Carbon itself is essential to life regarding its countless uses, and its emission into the atmosphere is a normal process. It eventually recycles from the atmosphere back to growing more plant life. Climate change merely occurs from too much of its presence in the atmosphere. More recycling itself can result in the atmosphere having more carbon. Twice as much recycling includes twice as much carbon unless the recycling is twice as fast. More than four times as much plant life could thus be needed to counter twice as much animal life unless more green energy is used in place of hydrocarbon fuels.

Disastrous effects of climate change have become more evident. Measure of average temperature at the equator resulting in more frequent and disastrous hurricanes and tornadoes has been increasing. Record flooding in 2017 from hurricanes in Texas caused billions of dollars' worth of damage along with human deaths. Such incidents along with record forest fires continue on Earth's surface.

There are possible means of preventing such disastrous outcomes of climate change. A well-known example is that of replacing automobiles powered by gasoline with electric vehicles. Such conversion seems to be increasing. Moreover, home owners can use solar energy to power their homes and electric vehicles, and it is possible they can even sell their electrical capture of solar energy to companies selling electricity to the general public.

A particular classification for a general remedy of climate change is Beaver Engineering. Beavers simply change the flow of water for their benefit. They create ponds of water by damming streams instead of allowing water to flow back to the ocean.

A historical example of Beaver Engineering is the Toman aqueduct construction that began in the third century BC. It was promoted by an invention of an arch and a large-scale inverted siphon of clay. Lead pipes were reinforced with stone blocks to allow water to flow on a large scale along a straighter path by means of gravity and water pressure. Even more scientific innovation allowed for more tunneling for underground aqueducts and water reservoirs that extended hundreds of miles from Rome. The Roman empire even extended its construction of them to other countries.

Beaver Engineering as remedies to climate change could be economically feasible in modern times in the sense of maintaining supply and demand with regard to production of food and other products of essential living conditions. Stored water in containers or underground reservoirs and aqueducts could enable more farmers to produce more food by means of having more water reserves and greenhouses.

A modern example is the development of desert land in eastern Oregon. There is less water supply due to its prevention by the Cascade mountains. Although land varies in its acidity, it is somewhat controllable by means of how it varies in crop production. Contrary to this eastern Oregon desert land is the Willamette valley west of the Cascades. It consists of highly nutritional soil whereby blackberries grow so rapidly that they are generally considered to be weeds in need of removal. Although the desert land of eastern Oregon is not as nutritious, there is various means of growing various crops in it. For instance, in some areas where the soil is slightly alkaline, it is more useful for growing such foods as pumpkins, asparagus, beets, cauliflower, celery, carrots and broccoli. Such foods as pumpkin seeds and broccoli provide needed nutrition for the brain to activate its subconscious memory. It depends on what nutrition the brain is lacking.

The area also has ample sunshine and wind for solar panels. Consider large and tiny windmill turbines that can catch wind from any direction. They can be made of cylinders divided equally of three parts whereby one of three sides encounters more direct wind from any direction. Smaller cylinders catch and process slower wind while larger ones catch and process faster and stronger wind. There is thus more variance potential for the capture of more useable wind energy.

The process of creating electricity was discovered in the mid-nineteenth century. It is simply that a variable magnetic field induces an electric current inside a wire that can itself be used to create more variance in the magnetic field and so forth. Its usefulness came later by use of dams converting the flow of river currents into electricity from the variance of magnetic fields.

Beaver Engineering is a possibility, but economic success is likely dependent on what can be produced in manner of creating an overall wealthier national economy. Government has invested in highways that provide easier transport of goods and services, but negative results have also occurred. For instance, the use of highways has resulted in use of carbon fuels increasing atmospheric temperature.

The use of carbon fuels has been acceptable by the general population. Government control of them is argued to be contrary to free enterprise. However, a counterargument is according to the question of what is the economic value of the air we breathe. Since there is enough supply for it being free to breathe, it has no positive economic value; it has only negative economic value in the sense of overcoming its destructive capability. However, even though financing of a government military for prevention of invasion by another nation is acceptable, financing against climate change is a lot less acceptable. A way for it to become more acceptable is with regard to having more positive economic results.

How can government investment in climate change result in more acceptance?

It could become more acceptable in view of a possibility of it resulting in more production of affordable products, but how that occurs is complex depending on what is used against present competition already established.

There have been great amounts of effort to reverse global warming. On the federal level, tax credits have been proposed for the purchase of electric vehicles. Water and electric utilities on state and county levels have offered to purchase electricity from home owners who produce it by way of solar panels. Home owners could even sell energy to the electric utilities. However, if such a process develops too rapidly, the price of electricity to customers of it could rise out of balance because of electric companies needing to cover the cost of production along with having fewer paying customers. Such change thus needs to gradually occur as feasible for positive effect on the economy unless government intervention somehow becomes more feasible for recovery of more present effect.

Population in support of combating climate has been increasing. Still, even more support could be beneficial to healthier living conditions. Free choice for economic competition of wealth is a natural deterrent open to debate. Penalizing carbon fuel products has resistance because of a threat to employment opportunity as well as countless owners of stocks in such fossil fuel production companies. A more social policy of persuading a cleaner production of energy could be in allowing it to be part of a feasible transfer over from carbon fuel production for companies along with their stock owners to profit instead of losing out. The social policy could also include indentured servants hired of people fleeing from threatening life conditions from those in control from where those freeing had escaped. It could require them to help produce additional product to maintain balance of supply and demand economics. With the production of air purifiers that can recycle carbon use, for instance, it could promote cleaner air in stores and homes for a healthier environment for us to live in. However, medical professionals and hospitals could also need to be compensated for if they then have less patients to heal.

Even so, the transfer over would likely be gradual enough to allow positive change to occur in manner of increasing credit as much as increasing more product of more demand by the same amount. No rapid inflation thus needs to occur if change is done right, which includes positive results.

Vehicles using electric energy instead of gasoline is a possible means of reversing climate change, but stored electricity can also be explosive. However, hazardous effects of climate change are also evident. Measure of the average temperature of ocean water at the equator has increased along with such effects as more frequent and disastrous hurricanes and tornadoes. Record flooding in 2017 from hurricanes caused billions of dollars of damage in Texas along with human deaths. Such results have continued along with record forest fires occurring in various locations. California, in particular, has been experiencing extreme weather resulting in devastating forest fires and flooding. Lives have been lost along with large amounts of houses and other property having been damaged. Disastrous storms have continued eastward past the Midwest into East America.

Other remedies that had been proposed more than a decade ago include carbon capture, reversing ocean acidity by adding iron to it, and spraying sulfuric acid into the air.

Regarding carbon capture, the general atmosphere contains only about one part carbon dioxide per two hundred and fifty parts of air. Its main contributors are automobiles, farms, houses and stores. With respect to houses and stores, an advanced air scrubber for carbon capture was proposed in 2009 by physicist Peter Eisenberger. The proposal was supported by his colleague Graciela Chichilnisky who had become educated in economics. However, although similar air scrubbers had already been established in power plants, and carbon also accumulates inside stores by the breathing of customers and employees, their proposal at the time was generally too speculative with the possibility of having disastrous side effects.

The Einsenberger method supposedly preferred to use steam at a lower temperature for lower cost efficiency, and Chichilnisky advocated capture of carbon dioxide be sold to such established users of it for resupplying oil wells and making carbonated beverages. A commercial plant to collect carbon dioxide from the air was operational in Switzerland in 2017 that preceded the planning to establish plants in the state of New York and elsewhere in 2018. The Switzerland plant even sold carbon dioxide to a nearby greenhouse for it to release oxygen back into the atmosphere.

Most carbon dioxide emitted into the atmosphere comes from such emissions as automobiles and animal life. The latter significantly includes us humans breathing within such large buildings as stores for shopping and other activities.

Although the outside atmosphere contains only about one part of carbon dioxide per two hundred and fifty parts of air, the Eisenberger method supposedly preferred the use of steam at a lower temperature for lower cost. Chichilnisky advocated the capture of carbon dioxide be sold to such established users for resupplying oil wells and making carbonated beverages. A commercial plant to collect carbon dioxide from the air was operational in Switzerland in 2017. A similar commercial plant in the state of New York had been planned to be available by 2018 along with several other plants elsewhere. The Switzerland plant sold carbon dioxide to a nearby greenhouse for increasing the growth of plants for their carbon absorption.

It is also noted that, in 2008, David Keith built a four-foot-wide structure with a twenty-foot height and a bottom fan for sucking in air. The air came out at the top of the structure with less than half as much carbon dioxide that had entered at its bottom. He also suggested spaying sulfuric acid into the lower stratosphere at the equator for winds to distribute it around the globe to reflect sunlight back into outer space. However, side effects were still not adequately understood, such as possible depletion of the ozone layer resulting in different weather patterns around Earth, and how to reverse possible error of calculation from lack of knowledge.

David Keith became president of a company named Carbon Engineering, and claimed in 2021 that it is economically feasible to produce gasoline from limestone, hydrogen and air by means of a vast network of air scrubbers. Although it is not itself expected to reduce a significant amount of excessive carbon, it could be a contributing factor.

Other proposed remedies have been that of reversing ocean acidity by adding iron to it, and by spraying sulfuric acid into the air.

Dispersing iron into the ocean was tried as somewhat more of a careless but successful speculation. It had become evident that ocean life is decreasing due to the acidity of too much carbon dioxide in the water, but not enough carbon was evident in colder waters. In 1992, a collapse of the Newfoundland cod fishery occurred. Too much fishing was blamed for its cause. However, in 2008, a volcano erupted on the Aleutian Islands resulting in the spread of volcanic ash over the Gulf of Alaska. An unusually massive number of phytoplankton, as an ocean food source whereby oxygen is emitted into the atmosphere, was noticed to have occurred after a few months, and a Frazer River run of Sockeye salmon followed about two years later. It was followed again in 2011 by about six million of them. The result indicated that the number of salmon in the ocean can be increased with an iron supplement. However, since it was against international law, there was also disapproval by scientists and the ire of environmentalists. Still, Russ George along with the Haidea Salmon Restoration Corporation conducted an experiment in 2012 to spread one-hundred tons of iron sulfate over an ocean eddy about three hundred miles from Queen Charlotte Islands of Canada. Phytoplankton formed months later within about a one-hundred-kilometer area that was followed in 2013 by about four times as much pink salmon.

As Ken Whitehead explained it in his article titled A Dangerous Experiment Gone Right, there tends to be a warm layer of ocean water over the deep colder water. There lacks a mixing of Phytoplankton needing iron for photosynthesis from the atmosphere for acquiring inorganic carbon. More carbon dioxide is then absorbed for the dead cells of phytoplankton to sink to the ocean bottom in allowing more collection of carbon from the atmosphere.

Although the experiment appeared to have been successful, more caution has still been advised regarding natural balance. Although the algae blooms of phytoplankton increase at a rapid rate from the photosynthesis of sunlight and the absorbing of nitrogen and phosphorous from iron, too much blooming also appears to starve fish in need of oxygen, and some types of algae are poisonous. Scientific studies thus appear needed for a continuous application of the procedure. It could be successful in the northern parts of the ocean with colder water, but most of the warmer ocean could now have too much carbon for negative effects to occur instead.

Another promising remedy of climate change is production of an agriculturally charcoal fertilizer known as biochar having historical background success. Whether knowledgeable or simply the usual way of farming and cooking at the time, it is evident that such practices produced enough biochar to have fertilized infertile soils of the Amazon about two thousand years ago. They are to this day still more fertile than neighboring soils that could also become more fertile with proper application of biochar.

In moder times, farmers burn fields of plant life remaining after their growing season to fertilize soil for next season. Forest fires similarly contribute to soil fertility for more tree growth. Biochar is created as conversion of hydrocarbons to fertile charcoal by way of heat within a range between about seven-hundred and nine-hundred degrees Fahrenheit. Still, Russ George along with the Haidea Salmon Restoration Corporation conducted an experiment in 2012 to spread one-hundred tons of iron sulfate over an ocean eddy about three hundred miles from Queen Charlotte Islands of Canada. Phytoplankton formed months later within about a one-hundred-kilometer area that was followed in 2013 by about four times as much pink salmon.

The benefits of biochar are not only that it enhances production of healthy food, there is less carbon added to the atmosphere regarding its natural process of recycling because of it having such long-term use as being part of lumber-built houses. Moreover, if forest waste is used to produce biochar, it could result in less forest fires and more controllable ones that, in turn could save billions of dollars per year while assisting in the reversal of climate change.

Biochar is simply a means of transforming waste into compost. Sawdust, for instance, can become effective compost after about two years of being ground cover. It first absorbs nitrogen from the soil and then gradually releases it back into the soil for the soil to become even more fertile. Biochar itself is about seventy percent carbon with the rest of it being mostly nitrogen, hydrogen and oxygen. It benefits the soil mainly by it absorbing, retaining and purifying water along with its fertilization. There is a nitrogen cycle whereby the chemical diversity of the biochar allows microbiological organs to process the nitrogen of infertile nitrate to a fertile one. It can be combined with other compost for even healthier results depending on the particular condition of the soil and what is to be grown. However, too much nitrate can also be harmful by helping produce poisonous algae.

Carbon itself needs to be used in proper manner. About one-two-hundredth of Earth's crust is carbon that forms into more compounds than any other element. One particular compound of pure carbon is graphite that normally occurs as black crystal flakes and masses of metamorphic rocks. It is extremely soft to be cleaned by means of less pressure producing less heat from resistance of the other material. Its efficient thermal stability allows electrical conductivity for such further usefulness to include electronics, lubrication, steelmaking, and so forth.

Regarding the atmosphere, it normally contains about seventy-eight percent nitrogen, twenty-one percent oxygen, less than one percent argon, and only one-twenty-fifth percent of carbon and menthane. Although the amount of carbon is extremely slight in comparison, its influence on the effects of other particle is tremendous because of its ability to combine with most other atomic particles including other carbon ones. Such ability can be either constructive or destructive. Investment in constructive uses either by government or freewill of the people should be more favorable.

Such social effort can be successful. The construction of the Grand Coulee dam in the state of Washington is a successful example. It has allowed for farming along with power to generate electricity to develop, in turn, a prosperous community after a time of severe poverty. To the contrary, allowing for a severe drought to maintain in Afghanistan resulted in farmers growing opium to survive. They became controlled by drug cartels and terrorists. Similarly, results have become routine in other areas controlled by monopolies and oligopolies either by them as political leaders or being in control of political leaders.

Regarding the latter, overcoming political resistance can possibly be achieved by investing in stocks according to free enterprise apart from government. There are companies in support of reversing climate change. With more disasters occurring from climate change, such companies are more prone for future success, and companies affected negatively by climate change could be more prone for future failure. Wiser stock investment could thus be in favor of companies providing support for reversing the increasing temperature of the atmosphere.

Support for combating climate change has been increasing, but more can be beneficial. Free choice for economic competition of wealth is a natural deterrent open to debate. Penalizing carbon fuel producers has resistance because of a threat to employment opportunity as well as countless stock owners of fossil fuel production companies. A possible remedy could be an open stock market for climate change solutions as well with regard to it having potential for more gradual creation of individual wealth along with more overall prosperity for both the rich and poor. As for overcoming resistance, a social policy of persuading cleaner production of energy could be in allowing it to be part of a feasible transfer from carbon fuel production to clean energy ones for owners of the former to profit instead of losing out. Everyone could thus benefit both economically and physically from proposed remedies of climate change according to stock exchange.

As for actual means of reversing climate change, other aspects of physics could also be useful. In a fiction movie of the future, for instance, someone flipped a coin-size metal into the air that resulted in soundful information. Today, we have computers storing and processing information merely by change occurring to the atomic structure of metal. A small computer plugin containing stored information of dozens of books is merely a small metal with plastic cover. As in relation to electric energy, it is further possible to create robots that can more efficiently perform duties more difficult for us humans to do by ourselves.

An essential condition relating to the combating of climate change is that of balance. It is not that the use of carbon is itself wrong; it is that too much use of it in a way it pollutes the atmosphere too much is wrong. Similarly, not enough consumption of carotene (Vitamin A) can result in us having blindness, baldness and even death. Balance is also conditional in the sense that some of us might require more of the carotene than others of us do. Remedies for both the natural cause and man-made cause of climate change are thus more subjectively complex. Science is needed for more of its future understanding.

What needs to be understood is that climate change is mainly critical regarding how much heat energy becomes stored in the atmosphere and how much of it needs to be reversed according to particular circumstances. An effective means of reversing global warming is to use the heat in a way that it does not immediately recycle back into the atmosphere as the same amount received from it. For instance, it can be converted to electricity and so forth by means of wind. The electricity can then provide enough energy to produce such carbon products as diamonds, steal and stronger wood for more durable construction needed against more hazardous weather.

Electric car batteries have remained a problem in that they are vulnerable to explosion and the start of fires, and there is still lack of recharging stations in many areas. Future remedies are possible and likely to occur by means of correction from trial and error. More innovation for improvement is still likely needed. Possibilities are here speculated similar to that of Beaver Engineering.

Development of civilization has occurred similar to Beaver Engineering. Along with farming there is more need of water control, which has been a main source of hydroelectricity development. Although dams can result in catastrophic flooding, they can also be more productive by means of proper control. Usage of it is according to need. Where there is more need of it, a greater amount water supply as natural storage of electric energy is needed for more use of it per time. Carbon along with other metals can be used to produce pipes to transport water stored in large tanks positioned high in the mountains. The flow of water through them can even produce electricity before reaching areas more in need of water for agricultural success.

The natural production of green energy has been a successful part economic development by means of social cooperation. Benoit Fourneyron (1802-1867) was a French engineer who developed the first hydropower turbine. It was implemented in 1895 as a commercial plant located at Niagara Falls at the border between Canada and the state of New York. Soon after, William Armstrong (1810-1900) built and operated at his own house in Northumberland, England his own private electrical power station. By 2019, hydroelectric power stations implemented by dams include about fifty percent of energy production of thirty-five countries.

The storage of water itself has multiple options for increasing wealth. A Poplar tree, for instance, is a particular hardwood that grows more rapidly than others just from a short branch that can root out in a glass of water. It can be used for such production as plywood, furniture and paper. It is a softer and lighter hardwood with more shock resistance. It also burns at a higher temperature than most other wood.

Stored water in containers or underground reservoirs and aqueducts could be used by such indentured servants as people fleeing from life threatening situations within other nations. At the southern border where there is of more drought, they could vaporize ocean water to grow poplar trees. With the use of horses that humans have socialized with for thousands of years, they could even transport their own ocean water. The survival of humans in particular drought areas had even dependent on the horse's extra ordinary ability to survive according to the great strength of their legs, stamina and so forth. They have socially bonded with us humans as loyal servants that care to serve as such for their life purpose. They could still be used to transport water and other needs.

There are scientific ways to create other forms of energy. Lasers can transform light by changing its wavelength into a particular one. Energy can also be transformed into particular light energy, as by a laser process, that is about ninety-five percent the same as sunlight that could be used in greenhouses to grow crops in otherwise areas that do not have enough natural light to do so.

Another natural element that can control temperature for less extra use of energy is bird feathers. Bird feathers filling the inside of blankets, as have been made as such in Taiwan, maintain the same temperature of our bodies at ninety-eight degrees Fahrenheit regardless of the difference in temperature outside the blankets. It is how birds endure freezing cold winters and hotter summers. As to the dying of chickens by either age or butchering for human food, their feathers could be used as well for a significant purpose. Moreover, similar to feathers, coats have been made as clothes used by astronauts in outer space for maintaining the same inside temperature similar to bird feathers maintaining it.

Such investments in the future need not result in more debt if more products are created in a way that there is more demand for and affordability to purchase them. Economic wealth is essentially product; money is merely a means of credit to facilitate such investment. More food and useful water coinciding with a healthier environment could result in fairer distribution of wealth that could further result in more prosperity and peaceful conditions among nations. It is a motivational factor that could prevent warlike escalation among different nations or of revolution within them.

Such investments in the future could pay for themselves in the present. Economic wealth is essentially product; money is merely a means of credit to facilitate such investment. More food, useful water and a more livable environment could result in a fair distribution of more wealth for the promotion of peace and prosperity.

One possibility is carbon capture. Some of us might feel more faintish while shopping in stores due to much carbon dioxide being breathed out by shoppers. Air purifiers could capture much of the carbon to be stored deep underneath ground for fertilization of soil. However, the heathier environment within stores might reduce the need for doctors.

Citizens of a nation can benefit from individual competition and social agreement. This principle can extend to nations themselves. They compete by production and trade. Some propose tariffs in order to balance out. If one nation takes advantage of poverty to use cheaper labor for production, as to bankrupt factories of other nations, then tariffs could be a means of protection. However, the process needs to be gradual enough to succeed without resulting in a depression. If done in more correct manner, more tariff income could offset less taxation income. As for more worldwide prosperity by social cooperation, an acceptable policy of combating climate change on the national order could be achieved in favor of peace and tranquility.

A POPULATION ISSUE
OF CONCERN

Although more animal population, including humans, contributes to more carbon dioxide in the atmosphere, human birth rates among nations have been declining. Reasons for it are complex. There is generally more decline among more poverty-stricken nations, and change in how women now compete for employment is another contributing factor.

More population of people on Earth could result in more disastrous effects than that of just polluting more carbon dioxide into the atmosphere. It could contribute to more poverty by means of having less land available for production of food and other commodities. However, the amount of rise or decline in population varies among nations.

China had become the second most populated nation on Earth in being exceeded only by India. In effect from 1979 to 2015, it established a birth control policy of a family only being allowed to have one child. It was allowed to have three children after that expiration date of 2015.

People of poorer living conditions tend to become more criminally activated in order to survive. Poorer nations tend to become more of a threat to wealthier nations. Social cooperation among nations could thus become more beneficial than mere individual competition among people themselves.

There has been a Chinese tendency to use cheaper slave labor for production of products to be sold to other nations, as fore there to become an export and import imbalance between products in such other nations as the USA. A counter measure is that of tariffs. Even though tariffs can provide government with income from trade rather than by taxation of local producers, as for maintaining a balanced budget and encouraging local production along with providing more labor opportunity, more remedies are in need for international cooperation among nations. Too much cost of tariff without enough time for national adjustment is more likely to result in recessions and even depressions among nations.

Part of the imbalance cause could be that of larger countries being able to transport cheaper goods. If a slight tariff had been in early place, it might have prevented such closure as food canneries having less need for their service.

Climate change could become another factor food production. Poorer nations now suffering from disastrous effects of climate change have become more open to the use of clean energy. With the use of solar and wind power for production of products, even cheaper slave labor becomes less needed.

Disastrous effects of climate change can themselves become deterrents to population increase. For its prevention, certain investments are needed. More convenient housing on less land could counter more homelessness. More stored water flowing downward through pipes could provide electrical energy along with the production of more needed food. As for the replacement of human labor with robots and so forth, more education is needed for citizens to know how to properly use them in a controllable manner.

There could also be such issues to consider as the right for having an abortion, and there is further consideration regarding difference between abortion and the prevention of pregnancy itself. Apart from it being either necessary or just a preferred alternative is the right to consume preventative medicine for the prevention of pregnancy from sexual pleasure.

Is sexual intercourse only needed for the birth of children or could it also be a means of pleasure? Should the decision be of government policy or of individual cooperation? It likely depends on the vote of citizens and their individual will to comply, and such compliance could eventually change along with climate change.

More specifically, it has been estimated that global population is expected to grow by two billion within the next sixty years into the eighties after reaching a high of about eighty billion. As for national comparison, one-fifth of nations, which include China, Italy, Spain and Southern Korea, now have land of lower fertility along with fewer birth rates.

Another factor of concern is the rise in age per person. Healthier living conditions can contribute to it, but climate change could counter it. Nations comparing to be ahead of climate change along with more stability conditions for longer age are more likely to have more economic success, but change in itself is still an issue of concern. Retirement income could become less available with fewer workers to contribute to it.
As robotic production increases, higher taxes of it could be needed to aid retirees in need of such production.

As for economics, success is partly dependent on land use and construction of facilities. Since climate change slowly occurs, prepared changes can be gradual as well. Anticipation of needed investment policy could include the need to preserve enough fertile land to grow enough crops.

Control of water flow could be essential. Underground pipes placed below rivers and streams flowing downward could use part of the water for electricity production, and they could further be used to store more useful water in other locations. The conversion of electricity to nearly that of sunlight could also be used for crop production inside buildings.

There is also space adventure to consider. What exist beyond Earth is not totally known. New discoveries could be made from space exploration, as for way to convert conditions on our moon and on other planets as more livable. Spaceships themselves could become livable colonies. Human life could thus expand beyond Earth depending on particular ways of investment.

Essentially needed could be more direct ways to prepare for change. With more vast destruction by tornadoes and so forth, more secure buildings, roads and so forth could be needed as a counter measure. Wealth among citizens could change. Those of us who are poorer tend to commit more crime in order to survive, even though some rich people tend to commit crimes either to become richer or prevent the risk of losing their wealth.

Presently populated cities could be more vulnerable to change, as to require more expensive development. Less populated areas, as in eastern Oregon could have less expensive opportunity. There is more open land for development by means of beaver engineering in a better way of combating climate change.

More technological advancement can be another factor. With such clean solar energy as sun and wind, living conditions could be created on and beneath ocean surfaces.

MY HEALTH ON EARTH

I was born in Childress, Texas in 1943. My father told me he was all-Texas quarterback his sophomore year in high school, but he then served in the army during WWII. He, my mother and older sister then moved to Oregon. After settling in the city of Eugene, he and my mother both worked to pay rent, and they tended social places later on that included alcohol consumption. Although my father became employed instead of furthering his education, my mother's brother became the Oregon University's fullback in football a few seasons in the 1950s. He later became a successful realtor.

My parents moved from one house to another about every two years. I became a loaner learning on my own. I learned fast and excelled at most everything I tried, but when I joined a baseball team, the son of the coach and son's friends played while I sat on the bench.

When younger, I tried smoking a cigarette. My mother caught me, made me swallow the smoke to convince me not to do it again. However, she did not quit and died in her sixties of cancer. Most all my relatives who smoked and drank alcohol died in their sixties. My father quit smoking in his forties and lived to be in his nineties.

I consumed a lot of salt and sugar while growing up. Along with such illnesses as measles, chickenpox and so forth, I had less stamina. Later on, I became too hyper from drinking coffee. Although its addictive effect lasted a couple of years, I was able to give it up by mere deter mination.

I had my tonsils removed when I was young. Later in life, I discovered I had acquired symptoms of cystic fibrosis, mainly being unable to gain weight after high school and having less upper fat in my body for my sweat glands to have less water for sweating. More saliva was being produced instead that became toxic in the form of allergies. Later in life, as in my seventies, my sinuses became clogged up for about five years. It suddenly cleared up after my sister lit a vanilla candle. I eventually realized that spring and summer pollen thickened my saliva and that vanilla was one ingredient that thinned it for it to do such goods things as clean teeth.

I also eventually discovered that tending to swallow more of the saliva before it accumulated too much was helpful. I no longer need to consume a little bit of vanilla-extract and try not to swallow because its odor being its effectiveness.

My double cousin, Donna Ticer, who had Huntington's Korea along with her older brother, father and grandfather, introduced me to nutrition. Although it did not cure her Huntington's Korea, it benefited me with having better health. However, other factors contributed to it as well. When a doctor told me my kidney stone was too big to pass and the prescribed opioid medicine did not reduce the pain, I decided to drink a large Pepsi. Right afterwards, there was no more pain and kidney stone found later on from the x-rays.

In my mid-seventies I began losing memory. I researched nutrition on the internet and came up with pumpkin seeds. After three weeks consuming only a tablespoon per day, I noticed improvement. Later on, I added broccoli to my diet and my memory improved even more. My memory is still not as good as it was in my younger days, but it has been improving. The brain does a lot and needs a lot of nutrition. However, what worked for me might not work for you. It depends on combination difference. For instance, after I consumed both an apple and orange within an hour apart, I soon had to get off the city bus to throw up in order not to suffocate from being clogged up. Certain healthy foods can combine to become unhealthy ones similar to how carbon can combine to result in hazardous effects of climate change.

I also incorrectly lifted while working in a cannery around the age of twenty. I came up with lower backpain that also affected my sensitivity around the neck. After treatment by a doctor, I did not give it enough time to heal. After retiring in my later years, I decided to give up driving and ride a bicycle instead. When I pushed on my heals instead of my toes, I noticed I had a lot less-lower backpain. I also began walking a lot. It enabled me to constipate more easily.

Just before reaching the age of 80, I rode my bicycle across town to the VA clinic. The nurse told me my examination indicated I am only in my twenties.